Microsoft® Office
Access® 2013:
Part 3

Microsoft® Office Access® 2013: Part 3

Part Number: 091006
Course Edition: 2.2

Acknowledgements

PROJECT TEAM

Author	Media Designer	Content Editor
Ken Hess	Alex Tong	Angie French
Gail Sandler		

Notices

DISCLAIMER

TRADEMARK NOTICES

Microsoft® Office Access® 2013: Part 3

Network Level

Network Level

About This Course

You've covered many of the basic functions of Microsoft® Office Access® and now you're ready to learn advanced Access features such as database management, advanced form design, packaging a database, encrypting a database, preparing a database for multi-user access, and more. Knowledge of these features separate database professionals from the casual database users or occasional designers. Today's training, added to that which you've gained from the previous two days, rounds out your Access education and provides you with marketable job skills.

You can also use the course to prepare for the Microsoft Office Specialist (MOS) Certification exams for Microsoft Access 2013.

Course Description

Target Student

Students taking this course are database administrators or prospective database administrators who have experience working with Access 2013 and need to learn advanced skills.

Course Prerequisites

To ensure your success in your course you should have experience working with Microsoft Access 2013, including a working knowledge of database design and creation, form design and creation, report design and creation, a working knowledge of database querying and the various table relationships. You can obtain this level of skill and knowledge by taking the following Logical Operations courses:

- *Microsoft® Office Access® 2013: Part 1*
- *Microsoft® Office Access® 2013: Part 2*

Course Objectives

Upon successful completion of this course, students will be able to:

- Customize a form layout to improve usability and efficiency of data entry.
- Add user interface features to validate data entry.
- Use macros to improve user interface design.
- Organize data into appropriate tables to ensure data dependency and minimize redundancy.
- Lock down and prepare a database for distribution to multiple users.
- Create and modify a database switchboard and set the startup options.

http://www.lo-choice.com

The LogicalCHOICE Home Screen

The LogicalCHOICE Home screen is your entry point to the LogicalCHOICE learning experience, of which this course manual is only one part. Visit the LogicalCHOICE Course screen both during and after class to make use of the world of support and instructional resources that make up the LogicalCHOICE experience.

Log-on and access information for your LogicalCHOICE environment will be provided with your class experience. On the LogicalCHOICE Home screen, you can access the LogicalCHOICE Course screens for your specific courses.

Each LogicalCHOICE Course screen will give you access to the following resources:

- eBook: an interactive electronic version of the printed book for your course.
- LearnTOs: brief animated components that enhance and extend the classroom learning experience.

Depending on the nature of your course and the choices of your learning provider, the LogicalCHOICE Course screen may also include access to elements such as:

- The interactive eBook.
- Social media resources that enable you to collaborate with others in the learning community using professional communications sites such as LinkedIn or microblogging tools such as Twitter.
- Checklists with useful post-class reference information.
- Any course files you will download.
- The course assessment.
- Notices from the LogicalCHOICE administrator.
- Virtual labs, for remote access to the technical environment for your course.
- Your personal whiteboard for sketches and notes.
- Newsletters and other communications from your learning provider.
- Mentoring services.
- A link to the website of your training provider.
- The LogicalCHOICE store.

Visit your LogicalCHOICE Home screen often to connect, communicate, and extend your learning experience!

How to Use This Book

As You Learn

This book is divided into lessons and topics, covering a subject or a set of related subjects. In most cases, lessons are arranged in order of increasing proficiency.

The results-oriented topics include relevant and supporting information you need to master the content. Each topic has various types of activities designed to enable you to practice the guidelines and procedures as well as to solidify your understanding of the informational material presented in the course. Procedures and guidelines are presented in a concise fashion along with activities and discussions. Information is provided for reference and reflection in such a way as to facilitate understanding and practice.

Data files for various activities as well as other supporting files for the course are available by download from the LogicalCHOICE Course screen. In addition to sample data for the course exercises, the course files may contain media components to enhance your learning and additional reference materials for use both during and after the course.

At the back of the book, you will find a glossary of the definitions of the terms and concepts used throughout the course. You will also find an index to assist in locating information within the instructional components of the book.

As You Review

Any method of instruction is only as effective as the time and effort you, the student, are willing to invest in it. In addition, some of the information that you learn in class may not be important to you immediately, but it may become important later. For this reason, we encourage you to spend some time reviewing the content of the course after your time in the classroom.

As a Reference

The organization and layout of this book make it an easy-to-use resource for future reference. Taking advantage of the glossary, index, and table of contents, you can use this book as a first source of definitions, background information, and summaries.

Course Icons

Watch throughout the material for these visual cues:

Icon	Description
	A **Note** provides additional information, guidance, or hints about a topic or task.
	A **Caution** helps make you aware of places where you need to be particularly careful with your actions, settings, or decisions so that you can be sure to get the desired results of an activity or task.
	LearnTO notes show you where an associated LearnTO is particularly relevant to the content. Access LearnTOs from your LogicalCHOICE Course screen.
	Checklists provide job aids you can use after class as a reference to performing skills back on the job. Access checklists from your LogicalCHOICE Course screen.
	Social notes remind you to check your LogicalCHOICE Course screen for opportunities to interact with the LogicalCHOICE community using social media.
	Notes Pages are intentionally left blank for you to write on.

1 | Implementing Advanced Form Design

Lesson Time: 1 hour, 30 minutes

Lesson Objectives

In this lesson, you will customize a form layout to improve usability and efficiency of data entry. You will:

- Add controls to forms.

- Create a subform.

- Organize information with tab pages.

- Access multiple forms from a single form.

- Apply conditional formatting.

Lesson Introduction

In Parts 1 and 2 of this course, you've learned some very important building blocks that now lead you into the more advanced features and capabilities of Microsoft® Access® 2013. One of those advanced features is creating forms that are not only professional but also engaging to the user.

The addition of controls, such as command buttons, adds extra functionality to your forms. You will edit the tab order of fields in your forms, work with the Anchoring tool, adjust your form's layout, create a subform, create tab pages and a Navigation form, and apply conditional formatting to your forms.

TOPIC A

Add Controls to Forms

You know add controls to a form. In this topic, you will rearrange the controls on a form and change the tab order to ensure that the users progress through the fields in a logical manner.

Controls

You add *controls* to forms to perform actions, to display a subset of data, to label data, to select options or to organize information. Most controls can be either bound or unbound. A bound control means that the information displayed or the selected information is directly connected to a table. In other words, the control is bound to data in a table. Unbound controls neither select data from a table nor do they insert data into a table.

Types of Controls

You can use several different types of form *controls* in Access 2013 that add efficiency and a professional touch to your forms. The following table lists the various form control types.

Control	Description
Text box	Used to display data or accept text input.
Label	Display descriptive text.
List box	Consist of rows of data that can be selected.
Command Button	Perform actions on demand.
Combo box	Combines functionality of a text box and list box.
Check box	Display a Yes/No value.
Option button	Display a Yes/No value.
Toggle button	Display a Yes/No value.
Option group	A group of check boxes, option buttons, or toggle buttons that provide a limited number of options to the form user.
—Tab Control	Several pages presented as a single set. ~~Form vs. Report~~
Hyperlink	Contains a URL link.
Insert Page Break	Lets you split the **Detail** section into separate pages.
Image	Holds link to an image.
Line	Lets you draw vertical, horizontal, or diagonal lines. Helps separate content graphically.
Rectangle	Lets you draw formatted rectangles around other controls. Helps content stand out.
Subform/ Subreport	Lets you insert a subform or subreport.
Unbound Object Frame	Lets you insert an unbound object frame.

Control	Description
Bound Object Frame	Lets you insert a bound object frame.
Attachment	Lets you add an attachment.
Web Browser control	Displays Web pages on a form.
Navigation Control	Allows the switching between various forms and reports with the creation of a navigation form.

Command Buttons

A command button is a control that's used to cause some action, such as closing the form you're working on or running a query. You can make a command button any size that you want and label the button with text or a picture.

 Access the Checklist tile on your LogicalCHOICE course screen for reference information and job aids on How to Add a Command Button to a Form

Calendar/Datepicker Control

The *Datepicker* gives you a choice of many formats or the ability to select the one that fits into your table data or that matches your preferred style. The Datepicker can be either bound or unbound. The Datepicker is actually a text box whose attributes are adjusted such that the calendar appears when selected. The user then selects or picks a date from a pop-up calendar.

 Access the Checklist tile on your LogicalCHOICE course screen for reference information and job aids on How to Add a Datepicker to a Form

Form Layouts

In Access, form and report layouts are quite similar. Many of the techniques, tools, and settings you have learned to use when laying out forms can be applied to report design.

When you create a new form from a query or table, the form that's created looks exactly like the table or dataset from which it was created. Sometimes this simple layout works, but often you'll want to change the layout to better suit screen resolution, design aesthetic, or practical functionality. For example, if you create a form from a table that has 30 fields from which your users need to supply data, they'll have to scroll down the page several times to see them all. This long page format can lead to frustrated users and skipped or incorrectly answered items. Rearranging the items on a page, shrinking or expanding fields, renaming fields and placing certain fields in a side-by-side configuration can greatly enhance the accuracy of data entry and the overall efficiency of your forms.

In the following example, you see fields that can be shrunk to more accurately represent the data contained in them, you see fields that would make more sense by being placed side-by-side and others that could be placed in different areas of a form page.

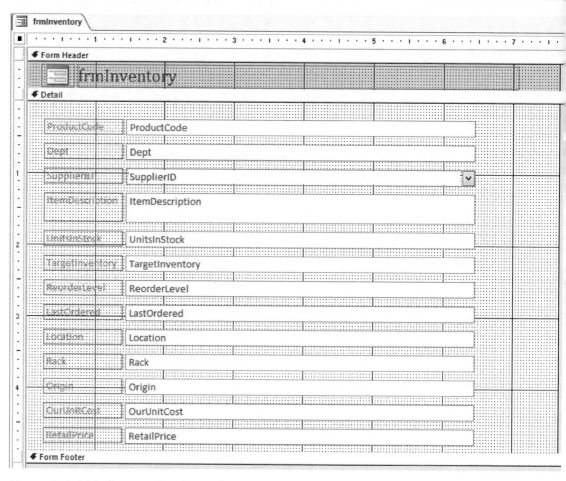

Figure 1–1: This form needs a better layout.

This form has a more visually appealing layout. It also would make it easier for users to enter data.

Figure 1-2: A better form layout.

 Access the Checklist tile on your LogicalCHOICE course screen for reference information and job aids on How to Adjust a Form's Layout

Quick Styles

Microsoft's Access 2013 designers have the busy database designer in mind with the inclusion of Quick Styles. Quick Styles are drop-down themed designs for your **Form** or **Report** command buttons that you can apply with a single click. Quick Styles are convenient and allow you to design command buttons with color and shape schemes consistent with the rest of your database.

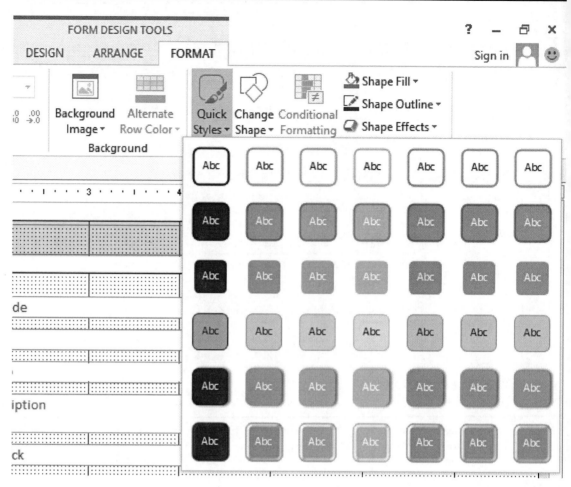

Figure 1-3: Quick Styles.

 Access the Checklist tile on your LogicalCHOICE course screen for reference
information and job aids on How to Apply Quick Styles to Form Controls

Tab Order

When you rearrange the fields on a form, depending on how significantly you moved the fields, you
might have altered the field *tab order*. The tab order is the order in which you navigate from field to
field on a form during data entry or if you were to tab through the fields using the **Tab** key on your
keyboard.

Change Tab Order

You can change the tab order of the fields to make the form easier and more intuitive when
performing data entry operations. Generally, top to bottom, left to right is the standard order.
However, this might not be true for all applications, therefore Access allows you to alter tab order
based upon your needs.

 Access the Checklist tile on your LogicalCHOICE course screen for reference
information and job aids on How to Change Form Tab Order

The Anchoring Tool

Form anchoring allows you to set form fields at a desired screen location. Access 2013 offers nine options for anchoring forms. When you adjust the form layout, you remove the anchoring from the form. You will want to set the anchoring again after you have adjusted the size and position of the fields on the form.

 Note: Be careful with the Anchoring tool, as it can drastically change the look of your forms and the ability for users to use them. **Top Left** is usually the best position for most applications.

Some of the Anchoring options result in fields overlapping or being repositioned so that they would be difficult to use. In most cases, you will want to use the **Top Left** Anchoring position.

 Access the Checklist tile on your LogicalCHOICE course screen for reference information and job aids on How to Use the Anchoring Tool to Set a Form's Screen Position

ACTIVITY 1-1
Changing the Tab Order on a Form

Data Files

C:\091006Data\Implementing Advanced Form Design\Inventory Database.accdb

Scenario

You are the web and database developer for Woodworker's Wheelhouse. To replace the current inventory system (the same pencil-and-paper system the company used in the 1950s), you have been creating an inventory database in Microsoft Access 2013.

Users have complained that after a recent form redesign that they can't efficiently work with the form due to the odd tab order. Many of the users have made mistakes that require hours of corrections and data re-entry. The request is for you to fix the form so that users can enter data by simply pressing **Enter** after their current entry to move to the next field.

---

1. Remove the layout from the Inventory Database.
   a) From the **C:\091006Data\Implementing Advanced Form Design** folder, open **Inventory Database.accdb**. If a security prompt is shown, select **Enable Content**.
   b) Save the file as *My Inventory Database.accdb* and select **Enable Content** if you are prompted.
   c) Open **frmInventory** in **Design** view.
   d) Press **Ctrl+A** to select all of the fields in the form.
   e) Select **FORM DESIGN TOOLS→ARRANGE→Table→Remove Layout**.

    Note: This course uses a streamlined notation for ribbon commands. They'll appear as "[Ribbon Tab]→[Group]→[Button or Control]" as in "select **Home→Clipboard→Paste**." If the group name isn't needed for navigation or there isn't a group, it's omitted, as in "select **File→Open**."

   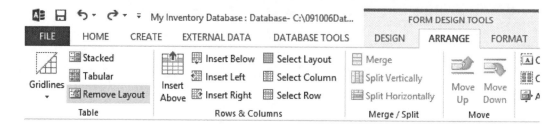

2. Arrange the fields to match the layout in the following graphic.

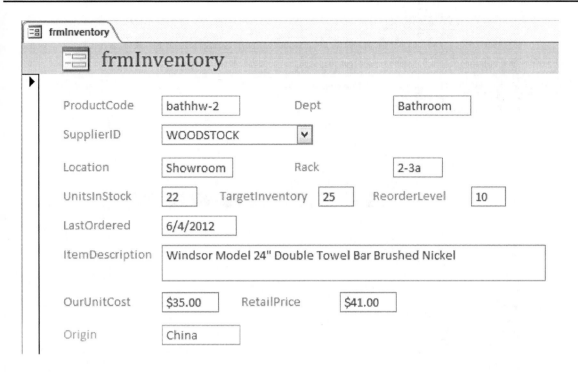

a) Resize fields appropriate to the data they contain.
b) Move fields to match the layout shown in the graphic.
c) Switch to **Layout** view to verify that the size and position of the fields is appropriate.

   In **Layout** view, data in the fields will help you determine if the field size and layout will work well. **Design** view doesn't show you the data, so it can be difficult to know whether the size and placement of fields will work for the data in your database.

3. Change the tab order.
   a) Switch to **Design** view.
   b) Select **FORM DESIGN TOOLS→DESIGN→Tools→Tab Order**.
   c) In the **Tab Order** dialog box, select **Auto Order** to change the tab order on the form to the standard top-to-bottom, left-to-right order.
   d) Select **OK**.
   e) Select **FORM DESIGN TOOLS→DESIGN→Tools→Tab Order**.
   f) Select the gray box to the left of **TargetInventory**. This grab point is where you select a field so you can move it up or down in the **Custom Order** list.

g) Drag **TargetInventory** up so it is between **Rack** and **UnitsInStock**.

h) Select **OK**.

4. Save and test the form.

a) Save the form.

b) Switch to **Form** view.

c) Press **Tab** several times to verify that the navigation between fields is top-to-bottom, left-to-right.

 Note: The **TargetInventory** field comes before the **UnitsInStock** field because you made a custom change to the order.

 Note: To explore naming conventions for Access databases and related objects, see the LearnTO **Set Up and Use a Naming Convention** presentation from the **LearnTO** tile on the LogicalCHOICE Course screen.

TOPIC B

Create Subforms

In Access, you can include subforms that link to the main form to report new or supplementary data that supports the main form. In this topic, you will create subforms.

Subforms

Subforms are independent forms that you add to existing forms that hold special data or additional data that you need to work with but that you need displayed differently on the body of the main form. For example, in **frmInventory**, the fields **OurUnitCost** and **RetailPrice** might be fields that you want shown on the main form but simple, single value fields aren't adequate. Subforms provide this visual and practical functionality.

 Access the Checklist tile on your LogicalCHOICE course screen for reference information and job aids on How to Create a Subform

ACTIVITY 1–2
Creating a Subform

Before You Begin

My Inventory Database.accdb is open, and frmInventory is displayed in **Form** view.

Scenario

Your manager has asked that you details about the suppliers your company uses to the Inventory form. You decide to create a subform on the **frmInventory** form so that users can see more details about the suppliers.

1. Place a subform on a form.
   a) Switch to **Design** view.
   b) Grab the top of the **Form Footer** bar and drag it down approximately one inch to make room in the **Detail** section of the Inventory form.
   c) Select **DESIGN→Controls→Subform/Subreport** 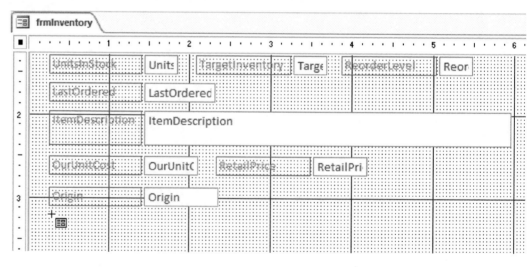. You might need to select the **More** button to see this control.
   d) In the **Detail** section of the form, under the **Origin** label, click in the form to place the **Subform**.

   The **Subform Wizard** opens.

2. Create the subform.
   a) If necessary, in the **Subform Wizard**, select **Use existing Tables and Queries** and then select **Next**.
   b) On the **Which fields would you like to include on the subform or subreport?** page, in the **Tables/ Queries** drop-down list, select **Table: tblSuppliers**.
   c) In the **Available Fields** list, double-click **SupplierID** to add it to the **Selected Fields** list box.
   d) Add **Company** and **ContactPhone** to the **Selected Fields** list box in that order.
   e) Select **Next**.
   f) On the **Would you like to define which fields link your main form to this subform yourself, or choose from the list below?** page, select **Next** to accept the default fields link.
   g) On the **What name would you like for your subform or subreport?** page, select **Finish** to accept the default name and close the wizard.

Note: When a subform is added to the form, it also adds a label. If you don't want the label to be displayed, you can delete it.

3. Save and test the subform.
   a) Save **frmInventory**.
   b) Switch to **Form** view.
   c) Scroll through the records using the navigation bar of the main form, **frmInventory**, and observe the changes.

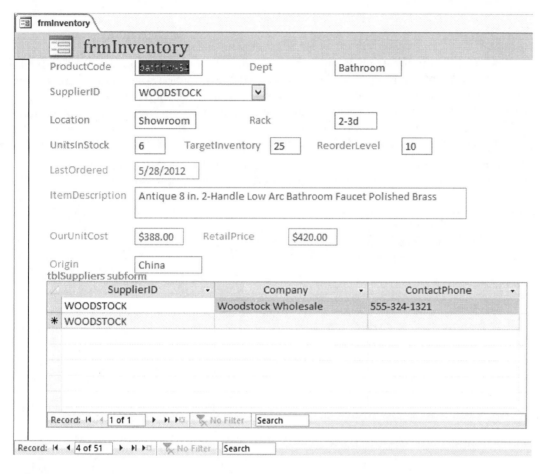

   d) Close the **frmInventory** form.

TOPIC C

Organize Information with Tab Pages

It's easier for users to enter required information if it's in manageable chunks. Tab pages provide that functionality, and also give the user the ability to flip back or forward during the data entry process. In this topic, you'll learn how to create tab pages.

Tab Pages

Tab pages or tabbed pages are an organizational unit useful for collecting and aggregating similar data onto separate forms, while enjoying the ability to switch easily among open forms via tabs. Tab pages also have the effect of making your forms look cleaner and simpler to the user. For example, if you want to create a medical history form, the first tab could be titled **Patient Information** and could hold general contact information such as name, address, and phone number. Subsequent forms could be titled **Insurance Information**, **Allergies**, **Family History**, and **Personal History**.

This separation of information makes it easier for the user to enter required information in manageable chunks, rather than on a page that's effectively three feet long.

 Access the Checklist tile on your LogicalCHOICE course screen for reference information and job aids on How to Use the Tab Control

ACTIVITY 1-3
Creating Tab Pages

Before You Begin
My Inventory Database.accdb is open.

Scenario
Your manager has requested a new form to display some limited supplier information. You have decided to use a Tab Control to separate the data into two tabs, with a tab for Supplier Info and a tab for Address.

---

1. Prepare to set a Tab Control on a new form.
   a) Select **CREATE→Forms→Blank Form** to create a new form.

   b) Switch to **Design** view.
   c) Select **DESIGN→Controls→Tab Control.** You might need to select the **More** button to see this control.
   d) Click in the form at the intersection of 1" and 1".
   e) Drag the resize handle down to the intersection of 5" and 5" to resize the tab control.

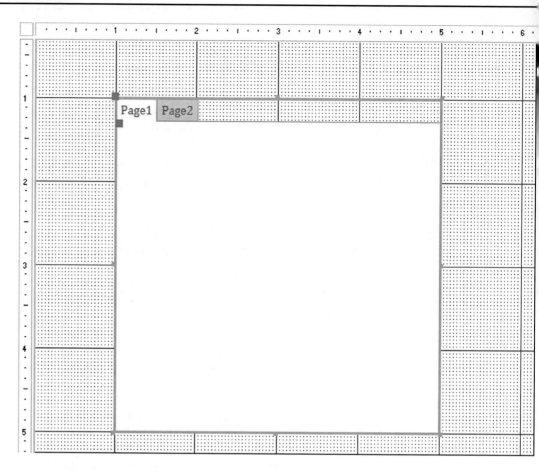

2. Assign tab names.
   a) Right-click the **Page 1** tab and select **Properties**.
   b) In the **Property Sheet** pane, select the **Other** tab.
   c) In the **Selection type:** drop-down list, select **Page1**.

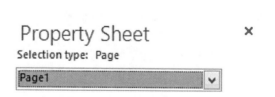

   d) In the **Name** field, type *Suppliers*
   e) In the **Property Sheet** pane, from the **Selection type:** drop-down list, select **Page2**.
   f) In the **Name** field, type *Address*

3. Add fields to the Suppliers page.
   a) On the form, select the **Suppliers** tab.
   b) In the **Property Sheet** pane, in the **Selection type** drop-down list, select **Form**.
   c) In the **Property Sheet** pane, on the **Data** tab, from the **Record Source** drop-down list, select **tblSuppliers**.
   d) Select **DESIGN→Tools→Add Existing Fields**.
   e) In the **Field List** pane, select **Company, ContactPhone, FirstName, LastName**, and **ContactEmail**. Remember, you can select multiple fields if you hold **Ctrl** and then click each of the fields.

f) Drag the selected fields on to the **Suppliers** page in the form.

4. Add fields to the Address page.
   a) On the form, select the **Address** tab.
   b) In the **Field List** pane, select **Address**, **City**, **StateProvince**, **Country**, and **PostalCode**.
   c) Drag the selected fields on to the **Address** page in the form.

5. Save and test the form.
   a) Save the form as *frmSuppliers*
   b) Switch to **Form** view.
   c) Scroll through the records to see that the fields on the form are populated with information from tblSuppliers.
   d) Close the **frmSuppliers** form.

TOPIC D

Enhance Navigation of Forms

Users find it easier to access related forms from a single location, rather than having to open multiple forms. Therefore, Access 2013 provides you with the ability to have a single form that links to multiple forms and reports.

Navigation Control and Navigation Forms

Access 2013 includes a Navigation Control that makes it easy to switch between forms and reports in your database. The Navigation Control can be added to an existing form, and a Navigation form is simply a form that contains a Navigation Control. In addition to helping with organizing forms and reports, a Navigation form is important if you plan to publish a database to the Web, because the Access **Navigation** pane does not display in a browser.

The Tab Control and Navigation forms provide similar functionality. Why would you use a Navigation form or control instead of a Tab Control? One reason is that the Navigation form and control provides a mechanism for supporting a hierarchy of options (enabling users to select a main category, and then select sub-categories), where the Tab Control does not.

In addition, the load-time behavior is different for the two types of controls. The Tab Control loads all its child objects as it loads. The Navigation form loads each child form or report on demand. This means that the Tab Control may take longer as it loads the data for all of the child objects before it is ready to use. The Navigation form loads the data as each item is selected, making the initial load time faster.

 Access the Checklist tile on your LogicalCHOICE course screen for reference information and job aids on How to Create a Navigation Form

ACTIVITY 1-4
Creating a Navigation Form

Before You Begin

My Inventory Database.accdb is open.

Scenario

Your manager has requested that you find a more convenient way for them to view the Inventory and Suppliers forms as they go back and forth between the two forms. Your manager also wants to quickly view all current reports so that can review them and determine if they are all necessary. You decide to create Navigation forms to accommodate these two requests.

---

1. Create a form and add the Navigation Control to display the Inventory and Suppliers forms.

   a) Select **CREATE→Forms→Blank Form** to create a new form.

   b) Switch to **Design** view.

   c) Select **DESIGN→Controls→Navigation Control**. <img> You might need to select the **More** button to see this control.

   d) Click in the form at the upper-left corner.

   e) In the form, in the Navigation Control, double-click the **[Add New]** tab, then type *Inventory* and press **Enter**.

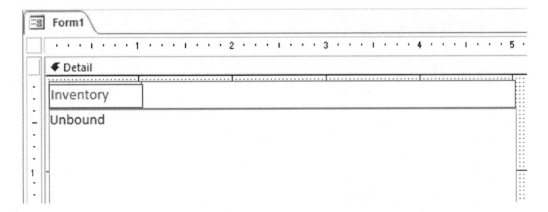

   f) If necessary, select **DESIGN→Tools→Property Sheet** to display the **Property Sheet**.

   g) In the **Property Sheet**, select the **Data** tab.

   h) In the **Navigation Target Name** drop-down list, select **Form.frmInventory**.

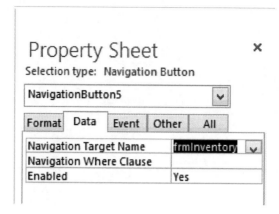

i)   In the **Property Sheet**, select the **Other** tab.
j)   In the **Name** box, type *Inventory*
k)   In the form, in the Navigation Control, select the **[Add New]** tab twice, and then type *Suppliers*
l)   With the **Suppliers** tab selected, in the **Property Sheet**, select the **Data** tab.
m) In the **Navigation Target Name** drop-down list, select **Form.frmSuppliers**.
n)   In the **Property Sheet**, select the **Other** tab.
o)   In the **Name** box, type *Suppliers*

2. Save and test the form.
    a) Save the form as *frmNavigation01*
    b) Switch to **Form** view.
    c) Scroll through the records on both tabs to see that forms **frmInventory** and **frmSuppliers** are displayed.

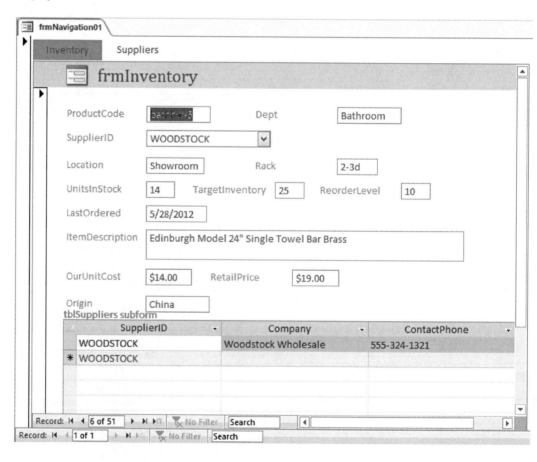

   d) Close the **frmNavigation01** form.

3. Create a Navigation form to display the Departments and ListOfOrders reports.
   a) Select **CREATE→Forms→Navigation→Vertical Tabs, Left** to create a new form.

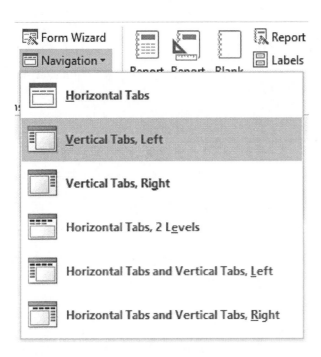

   b) In the form, in the Navigation Control, double-click the **[Add New]** tab, then type *Departments* and press **Enter**.
   c) Select **DESIGN→Tools→Property Sheet** to display the **Property Sheet**.
   d) In the **Property Sheet**, select the **Data** tab.
   e) In the **Navigation Target Name** drop-down list, select **Report.rptDepartments**.
   f) In the **Property Sheet**, select the **Other** tab.
   g) In the **Name** box, type *Departments* and then press **Enter**.
   h) In the form, in the Navigation Control, select the **[Add New]** tab twice, and then type *ListOfOrders*
   i) In the **Property Sheet**, select the **Data** tab.
   j) In the **Navigation Target Name** drop-down list, select **Report.rptListOfOrders**.
   k) In the **Property Sheet**, select the **Other** tab.
   l) In the **Name** box, type *ListOfOrders*

4. Save and test the form.
   a) Save the form as *frmNavigation02*
   b) Switch to **Form** view.
   c) View both tabs to see that reports **rptDepartments** and **rptListOfOrders** are displayed.

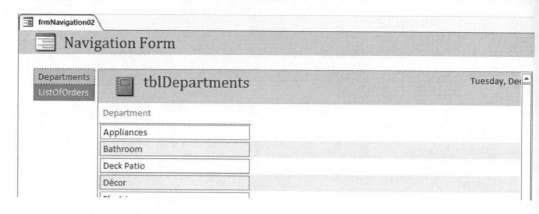

d) Close the **frmNavigation02** form.

TOPIC E

Apply Conditional Formatting

One way to make information stand out is to apply conditional formatting when specific criteria are met. In this topic, you will apply conditional formatting to your data to make it stand out in forms and reports.

Conditional Formatting

Conditional formatting is a feature of Microsoft Access that allows you to apply special formatting to data when a particular criterion is met. The criterion is manually set by the database administrator to highlight or to differentiate data in a form or report.

To create a criterion or condition for special formatting, you use the **Conditional Formatting Rules Manager** dialog box. Using this dialog box, you can define a range or build an expression to set up your *conditions*. For example, you might want to change the font color to red when an item's inventory falls below a certain number.

 Access the Checklist tile on your LogicalCHOICE course screen for reference information and job aids on How to Apply Conditional Formatting

ACTIVITY 1-5
Changing the Display of Data Conditionally

Before You Begin
My Inventory Database.accdb is open.

Scenario
The Sales Manager wants you to change the **Inventory** form to show when units in stock have fallen below reorder levels by changing the **UnitsInStock** field to red.

1. Apply conditional formatting to the **UnitsInStock** field.
   a) Open **frmInventory** in **Design** view.
   b) Right-click the **UnitsInStock** field and select **Conditional Formatting**.

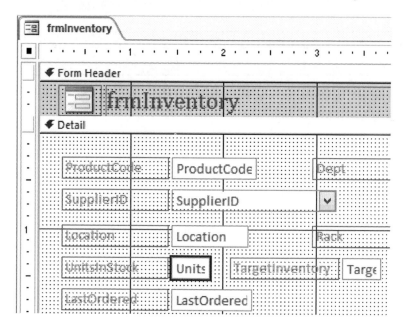

   The **Conditional Formatting Rules Manager** dialog box opens.
   c) Select **New Rule**.
   d) Verify that **Select a rule type** is set to **Check values in the current record or use an expression**.
   e) If necessary, in the **Edit the rule description** section, set the first box to **Field Value is**.
   f) Set the second box to **less than or equal to**.
   g) In the third box, type *[ReorderLevel]*
   h) From the **Font Color** drop-down list, select **Red**.

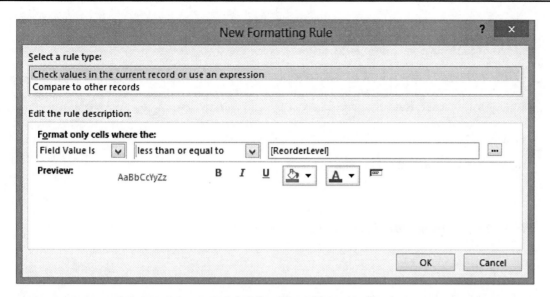

i) Verify that the text in the **Preview** section looks correct.
j) Select **OK** to close the **New Formatting Rule** dialog box.
k) Select **OK** to close the **Conditional Formatting Rules Manager** dialog box.

2. Save and test the form.
   a) Save the form.
   b) Switch to **Form** view.
   c) Navigate through the records.
      Any **Units in Stock** numbers that are less than the **Reorder Level** show up in red text in the form.

   d) Close the form and database.

Summary

In this lesson, you learned how to add controls to forms. Controls are essential to creating an easy-to-use and professional database application. The idea behind controls is to make the application pleasant for the user. Buttons, graphs, tab order, and subforms make the user feel as if he or she is using a piece of commercial-quality software. You also organized forms with tabbed pages and Navigation forms, and applied conditional formatting to data.

Why is tab order important in form design?

What is the purpose of adding command buttons to forms?

 Note: Check your LogicalCHOICE Course screen for opportunities to interact with your classmates, peers, and the larger LogicalCHOICE online community about the topics covered in this course or other topics you are interested in. From the Course screen you can also access available resources for a more continuous learning experience.

2 | Using Data Validation

Lesson Time: 1 hour, 10 minutes

Lesson Objectives

In this lesson, you will add user interface features to validate data entry. You will:

*   Constrain data with field validation.

*   Perform form and record validation.

Lesson Introduction

Being a database user is very different from being a database designer. Users don't know what you had in mind when you created the database, nor should they. A user should be able to open your database, without any knowledge of its inner workings, and productively enter data into it and query it without a great deal of detail about which type of data goes where. That's your job as a designer. If you've ever worked with a database that someone else designed, you probably noticed that some of the data was out of place or incorrect for the field. For example, you might have seen a city name where a street address belonged.

Data inconsistency can lead to wasted time and wasted money for you if you have to find and correct data entries on a regular basis. The answer to the problem is to implement a data validation plan. By using data validation techniques such as input masks, lookup lists, and form controls, database users won't be able to enter inconsistent data. One example is zip code information. Zip codes are numbers only. What if you had no data validation rules in place and a user enters "abcde" into a zip code field rather than "12345?" The results can be disastrous, if that information is tied to billing or customer information. You can see how important consistent data is to a database and to its users.

TOPIC A

Field Validation

Field validation will help users to enter correct data the first time around. In this topic, you'll employ some methods to enforce field validation.

Field Validation

Field validation refers to using the fields in the database tables to constrain the data entered into them. To use these field constraints, you must use the field properties, use input masks, or use lookup lists. Each validation method uses a different approach to data constraint. Which method you use is a matter of appropriateness for the field data. For example, to limit a zip code to five numbers or five numbers, a hyphen and four numbers (for extended zip codes) works for numeric data. However, constraining a **Last Name** field to letters only works for text data.

Field Properties

Every field in a table has associated properties. To view the properties for a field, switch to **Design** view, and select a field from the **Field Name** list.

tblInventory		
Field Name	**Data Type**	
ProductCode	Short Text	
Dept	Short Text	
SupplierID	Short Text	
ItemDescription	Short Text	
UnitsInStock	Number	
TargetInventory	Number	
ReorderLevel	Number	
LastOrdered	Date/Time	
Location	Short Text	
Rack	Short Text	
Origin	Short Text	
OurUnitCost	Currency	
RetailPrice	Currency	

Field Properties

General | Lookup

Field Size	Long Integer
Format	
Decimal Places	Auto
Input Mask	
Caption	
Default Value	
Validation Rule	
Validation Text	
Required	No
Indexed	No
Text Align	General

Figure 2–1: Field Properties for a Number data type field.

You can manually edit field properties or work through wizards for some of the options to guide you.

 Access the Checklist tile on your LogicalCHOICE course screen for reference information and job aids on How to Set Field Validation Rules

Input Masks

An input mask is a format for data entry. Its use dictates how data can be entered into a table. For example, if you want your data entry clerks to enter a phone number into a table, you could use a mask such as: (___) ___-____. This mask forces the person entering data to enter a ten-digit phone number into the field and the parenthesis and dash are included automatically. Input masks only work with text and date/time data types. Although a phone number is a number, it isn't a proper number and so a phone number field should be defined as text in your tables. Input masks may be entered manually or with the **Input Mask Wizard**.

The Input Mask Wizard

The **Input Mask Wizard** steps you through the process of creating an input mask for your field data. Some of the more common input masks are provided for you in the wizard. Phone number is one of them. You can even try out the pre-built input masks for yourself in the wizard before you commit to one.

Input Mask Characters

How would you prevent a data entry clerk from entering letters into your phone number field, since it is a text data type? Nothing will prevent it unless you define your input mask characters such that the clerk may enter numbers only.

Access includes some pre-built input masks. The pre-built input mask for phone number is (!\(999") "000\-0000;;_). It uses the number 9 for the area code portion of the phone number. This means that the data entry person could choose to enter nothing for the area code. If you want to require that users enter the area code, you will have to manually replace the 9s with 0s to ensure that numbers are entered for the area code.

Each of the characters in an input mask has a specific purpose. The following table lists the characters and the function they provide in the input mask.

Character	Description
0	User must enter a digit (0 to 9).
9	User can enter a digit (0 to 9), but is not required to do so.
#	User can enter a digit, space, plus sign, or minus sign. If skipped, Access enters a blank space.
L	User must enter a letter.
?	User can enter a letter, but is not required to do so.
A	User must enter a letter or a digit.
a	User can enter a letter or a digit, but is not required to do so.
&	User must enter either a character or a space.
C	User can enter a character or a space, but is not required to do so.
. , : : - /	Decimal and thousands placeholders, date and time separators. The character you select depends on your Microsoft Windows regional settings.
>	Converts all characters that follow to uppercase.
<	Converts all characters that follow to lowercase.
!	Causes the input mask to fill from left to right instead of from right to left.
\	Characters immediately following will be displayed literally.
""	Characters enclosed will be displayed literally.

Lookup Lists

A lookup list is a collection of values that restrict the choices for a particular field. The list source can be a query, a table, or a manually created custom list. The list can display more than one column of data, but only one column is used when the user selects a value. A good example is the list of states and their abbreviations. In your form, you might want to display the full state name and the abbreviation but only keep the abbreviation as the data.

The Lookup Wizard

The **Lookup Wizard** assists you in selecting a table or query, or in creating your own custom list for use in data entry. If you are creating the list based on a table or query, you can specify the order in which the list is sorted. If you are creating a list from within the wizard, the items will appear in the order you enter them.

List items from a table or query can be composed of one or more columns. You can resize the default column width to a width appropriate for the data being displayed.

You can allow users to make a single selection from the list or allow them to select multiple list items. If users are allowed to select multiple items, instead of just a text list, the items will be displayed as a check box list.

 Access the Checklist tile on your LogicalCHOICE course screen for reference information and job aids on How to Use the Lookup Wizard

Expression Builder

The *Expression Builder* is not a wizard. It is an open field where you manually create expressions to carry out a comparison, enforce a validation rule, calculate a value, or check data integrity. It uses a combination of expression elements, table fields, expression categories, and expression values. You might use any or all of those components in an expression.

Expressions can be very simple or quite complex. The following list shows a very simple expression and a very complex expression:

- > 1
- LIKE "[A-Z]*@[A-Z].com" OR "[A-Z]*@[A-Z].net" OR "[A-Z]*@[A-Z].org"

 Note: You will often see the term, "valid expression" when using the Expression Builder in Access. A valid expression refers to any mathematically valid expression, such as the following: >10, [Field1]/[Field2], [Field1] > [Field2] or ([Field1] + [Field2]) < [Field3]. If you use field names in your expressions, be sure that the fields contain numeric data and are of the Number data type.

ACTIVITY 2–1
Validating Data with a Field Property

Data Files

C:\091006Data\Using Data Validation\Inventory Database.accdb

Scenario

When entering new products into the Inventory database, users often make the mistake of entering a reorder value less than five, which is the minimum reorder number for any product. Your manager has requested that you fix it on the database side so that no one may enter a number less than five for any product reorder level.

1. Display the **Expression Builder** dialog box to set validation on the **ReorderLevel** field.

    a) Open **C:\091006Data\Using Data Validation\Inventory Database.accdb**. If a security prompt is shown, select **Enable Content**.

    b) Save the file as *My Inventory Database.accdb* and select **Enable Content** if you are prompted.

    c) Open **tblInventory** in **Datasheet** view.

    d) Select the **ReorderLevel** column.

    e) Select **TABLE TOOLS→FIELDS→Field Validation→Validation**.

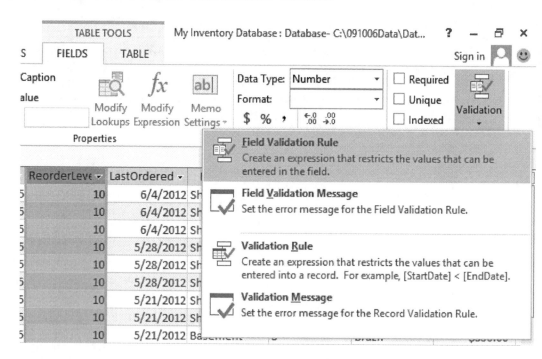

    f) Select **Field Validation Rule**.

2. In the **Expression Builder**, in the **Enter an Expression to validate the date in this field** text box, type *>4* and then select **OK**.

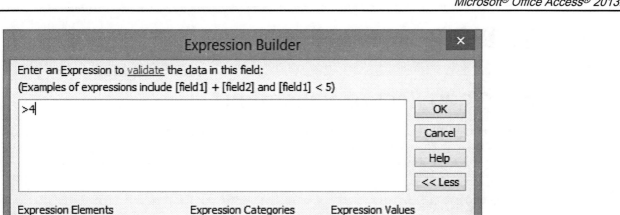

3. Test the validation.
   a) Save and close the table.
   b) Open **frmInventory**.
   c) Create a new blank record.
   d) In the **ReorderLevel** field, type *3* and then press **Tab**.
   e) Observe the error message that states that one or more values are prohibited by the validation rule of '>4'. Select **OK**.

   f) In the **ReorderLevel** field, type *5* and then press **Tab**.
      No error is displayed because 5 is a valid value for this field.

4. Close the form without saving.
   a) Close the form.
   b) If you receive an error message about needing to enter a value in the **tblInventory.ProductCode** field, select **OK**.
   c) If you receive an error message about not saving the record, select **Yes**.

TOPIC B

Form and Record Validation

Form validation allows you restrict even more to further decrease the amount of incorrect data. Record validation enables you to check the integrity of a record as it is being entered into a database object. In this topic, you will use a combo box to limit the options users have for entering data.

Form Validation

Form validation is similar to field validation in that you can manually enter expressions or build them with the Expression Builder. The difference is that you can further restrict data entry with form validation. Designers who want to add more data integrity validation may do so by using Control wizards for combo boxes, list boxes, and option groups.

Control Wizards

Control wizards are wizards that step you through the process of creating controls and restricting data along the way. You have to enable Control wizards to appear when you select a control that has an associated creation wizard. You must open a form in **Design** view to use the Control wizards.

The Combo Box Control

The combo box is a special form control that allows you to supply users with a list of choices when entering data, but also allows the user to type in a value if a suitable isn't found in the list. You can select **Limit to List** in the **Combo Box** properties, which will prevent any foreign entries. Combo boxes may be bound or unbound to data.

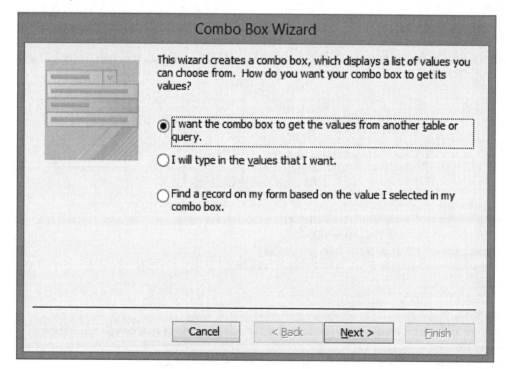

Figure 2–2: Selecting the type of combo box for a form.

Remember or Store Values

In the **Combo Box Wizard**, you specify whether to remember the value for later use or store the value in a field. If you are going to be using the value the user selects in the combo box to perform a task, you will want to select the option for Access to remember the value. If you want to store the value in your database, you need to select a field in which to store the value.

 Access the Checklist tile on your LogicalCHOICE course screen for reference information and job aids on How to Add a Combo Box Control

The List Box Control

A **List Box** control is a control that's similar to a combo box but does not allow values other than those displayed in the list. List boxes also display multiple rows, so their placement on a form is more critical than that of a combo box. A list box can be bound or unbound to data.

The Option Group Control

The **Option Group** control is a form control that is composed of option buttons, toggle buttons, or check boxes. Users may only select one choice from an **Option Group** control. One of the options can be set as a default option. For example, if you offer customers three shipping methods and only one option is available, an **Option Group** control would be appropriate.

 Access the Checklist tile on your LogicalCHOICE course screen for reference information and job aids on How to Add an Option Group Control

Record Validation

Record validation is similar to field validation in that you're using expressions to check data before it's saved to the database to ensure its consistency with corresponding data and to maintain reasonable conditions. Record validation occurs between fields in the same table. For example, if your Orders table contains a **ShippedDate** field and an **OrderDate** field, you want to be sure that the **OrderDate** is before the **ShippedDate**. The way to perform this check is to use record validation. Such an expression might look like this: [OrderDate]<=[ShippedDate]. If a user accidentally enters a date older than the order date, the user will receive an error.

 Access the Checklist tile on your LogicalCHOICE course screen for reference information and job aids on How to Create a Record Validation Rule

ACTIVITY 2-2
Using a Combo Box Control to Limit Option Values

Before You Begin

My Inventory Database.accdb is open.

Scenario

When users enter new items into My Inventory Database, they often don't enter the correct storage or display location for the item. You plan to create a list of the all possible locations so that the users may select the correct one. You want to enable wizard controls to assist you when you add this and other controls to forms.

---

1. Enable Control wizards.
   a) Open **frmInventory** in **Design** view.
   b) Verify that the **FORM DESIGN TOOLS→DESIGN→Controls→More→Use Control Wizards** is enabled.

2. Add a **Combo Box** control to the form.
   a) Delete the **Location** field from the form.
   b) Select **FORM DESIGN→TOOLS→DESIGN→Controls→Combo Box**.
   c) Click the form where you deleted the **Location** field to add the **Combo Box** control to the same location in the form.

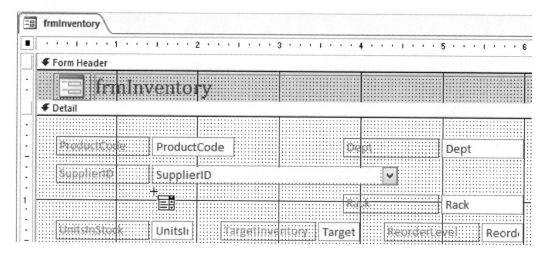

3. Use the **Combo Box Wizard** to add values to the **Location** field.
   a) In the **Combo Box Wizard**, select **I will type in the values that I want**, and then select **Next**.
   b) In the **Col1** column, in the first row, type *Showroom* and then press **Tab**.

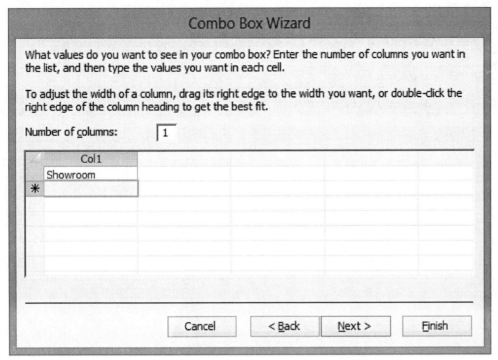

c) Add additional values: *Basement*, *Mill*, **Shed A**, **Shed B**, and **Shed C**, and then select **Next**.

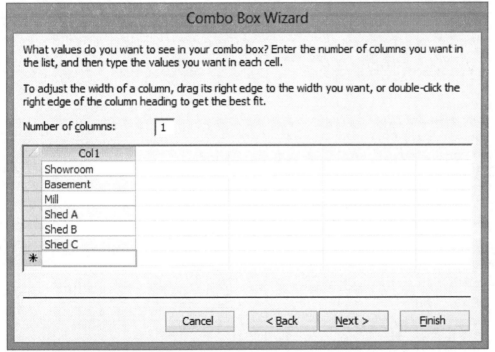

Hit Totals for Group by

d) Select **Store that value in this field**, and then from the drop-down list select **Location**.

e) Select **Next**.

f) In the text box, type *Location* as the label name, and then select **Finish**.

 Note: Depending on where you clicked on the form, you may need to move the new **Location** label and combo box.

4. Save and test the form.

a) Save the form.
b) Switch to **Form** view.
c) Select the **Location** field drop-down arrow to verify the options you added are listed.

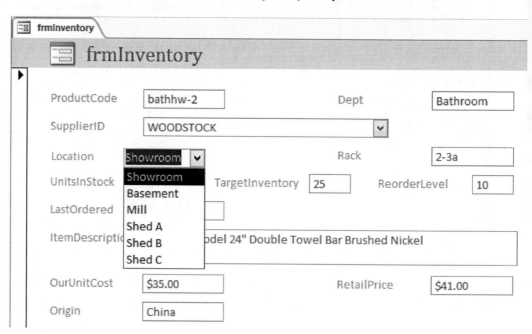

d) Close the form and the database.

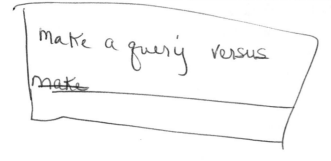

make a query versus make

Summary

In this lesson, you learned various data validation techniques to increase the integrity of your data and to minimize mistakes and errors in data entry. Data validation rules might slow the data entry process, but they will ensure accuracy.

Why should you apply data validation rules to every data point in your databases?

Is it reasonable to use form validation and record validation on the same table of data? If so, why?

 Note: Check your LogicalCHOICE Course screen for opportunities to interact with your classmates, peers, and the larger LogicalCHOICE online community about the topics covered in this course or other topics you are interested in. From the Course screen you can also access available resources for a more continuous learning experience.

3 | Using Macros to Improve User Interface Design

Lesson Time: 1 hour

Lesson Objectives

In this lesson, you will use macros to improve user interface design. You will:

- Create macros.

- Restrict records using a condition.

- Validate data using a macro.

- Automate data entry using a macro.

- Convert a macro to VBA.

Lesson Introduction

You have seen how you can make data entry easier for users with things like lookup lists, combo box controls, and validation. Another useful feature in Microsoft® Access® is to use macros to perform repetitive tasks or actions that are difficult for users to perform.

TOPIC A

Create a Macro

In this topic, you will learn to create macros to automate actions, to trigger events, to restrict records, to validate data, and to automate data entry. You will also create standalone macros and embedded macros.

Macros

Macros are pseudo-programs that perform a list of actions based on a set of instructions. Programmers prefer Visual Basic for Applications (VBA) and see macros as a simple alternative or a shortcut to real programming. This opinion has persisted since macros first appeared in Access 1.0. Macros are a good alternative to learning a complex programming language to perform relatively simple tasks. You can use macros to perform repetitive tasks or tasks that require an action that isn't easily duplicated by a user. Some examples of useful macros are opening and closing database objects, filtering forms and reports, starting wizards and dialog boxes, and performing some action on startup.

There are two general types of macros: event (embedded) macros and named (standalone) macros. Event macros are those that are triggered by an action. Named macros are macros that are called by name.

The Macro Builder Window

The Access 2013 *Macro Builder* or macro designer uses formal program construction, known as top-down flow. Top-down refers to the concept that a program begins at the top of the page and parses down the page in normal left-to-right reading fashion.

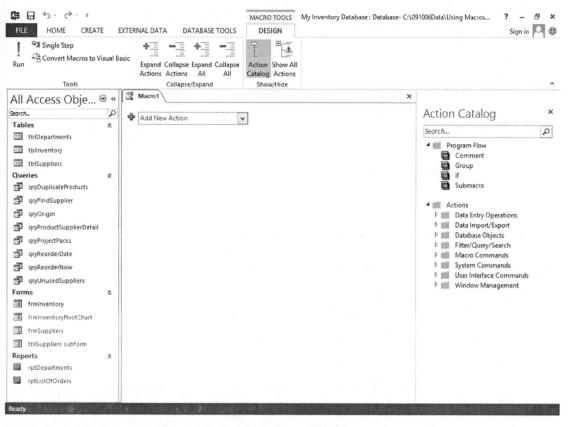

Figure 3-1: The Macro Builder window and Action Catalog.

When you open the Macro Builder, you're ready to begin adding actions. There are two ways to add actions to your macros. The first is to use the **Add New Action** drop-down list, select an action from the list, and then enter any required conditions or arguments into provided fields. The second is to use the Action Catalog to select macro actions to add to your macros. Expand the **Action** categories until you find the action you want, and drag it into the **Macro** pane, or double-click the action to add it into the **Macro** pane.

When you first open the Macro Builder, you might not see **Add New Action** in the drop-down list, but when you click into that pane, the words will display. You can reposition actions by dragging them to the new location once they are placed into the **Macro** pane. Alternatively, you can use the arrows to move actions up or down in the **Macro** pane.

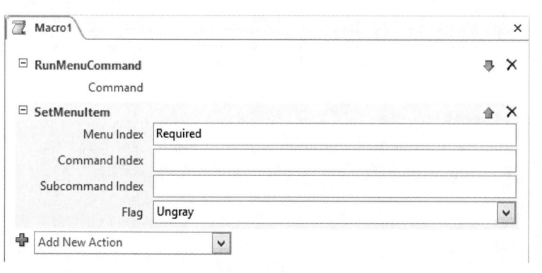

Figure 3-2: Macro Actions and Positioning Arrows.

To remove an action from the **Macro** pane, select the **Close (X)** control. You edit a macro action by giving it focus. Once you change focus to another action, any arguments or conditions are shown for easy reference.

Macro Actions

The purpose of a macro is to cause something to happen—an *action*. Therefore, macros are made up of actions. You can have as few as one action and a maximum of 999 actions in a single macro.

Types of Macro Actions

There are eight major macro action types. Those eight types are action groups whose members have similar functions. These macro actions are found in the Action Catalog. The following table identifies the eight macro types and their general functionality.

Macro Action	Functionality
Data Entry Operations	Delete, edit, and save records.
Data Import/Export	Outlook and Word import and export options.
Database Objects	GoTo, Open, Print, Repaint, Select, and Set.
Filter/Query/Search	Filers, searches, and shows records.
Macro Commands	Cancel, clear, remove, run, set, start, or stop macros.
System Commands	Beep, close, hourglass, and quit.
User Interface Commands	AddMenu, BrowseTo, MessageBox, NavigateTo, Redo, SetMenuItem, and Undo.
Window Management	Close, maximize, minimize, move, or restore a window.

Action Arguments

Argument is a programming term that refers to a bit of information that directs an action. When you give someone directions to the mall, you might say something like, "Go two miles East and then go one mile South." The action is "Go," and the arguments are two miles, East, one mile, and South. The arguments for the Go action are distance and direction.

Macro action arguments are the parameters an action uses to perform that action. For example, if you use the **OpenForm** action, one of the arguments must be the name of the form to open. For the **GoToRecord** action, one of the arguments is the name of the form, table or query you want to use as a record source. Another argument for the **GoToRecord** action is which record you want to go to: previous, next, first, last, new, or go to a specific record expressed as an offset from the current record.

Object Events

A macro is a collection of code that performs some action or actions for you. You can use a macro in a number of ways to perform those actions. An object *event* is an action triggered by a user on a database object—objects such as forms, reports and controls.

2nd part of developing

When do you want it to run Click of a field?

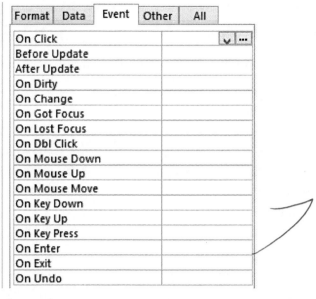

Format	Data	Event	Other	All

On Click	
Before Update	
After Update	
On Dirty	
On Change	
On Got Focus	
On Lost Focus	
On Dbl Click	
On Mouse Down	
On Mouse Up	
On Mouse Move	
On Key Down	
On Key Up	
On Key Press	
On Enter	
On Exit	
On Undo	

Figure 3–3: Event options for a form field.

Event Group	Description
Window Events	Opening, closing, or resizing a window.
Data Events	Updating or deleting records or any data.
Focus Events	Activating, entering, or exiting a field.
Keyboard Events	Pressing or releasing keys.
Mouse Events	Clicking or double-clicking the mouse.
Print Events	Format and print.
Error and Timing Events	An error or a lapse of time between records.

Events and Macros

When you attach a macro to an event, you're associating macro actions with some user action. For example, when a user tabs from one field to another, the act of pressing the **Tab** key on the keyboard to move from one field to another is an event. Attaching a macro to that event can perform some automated action, such as closing the form, opening another form or setting the Recordset to **New** so that you can enter a new record automatically.

 Access the Checklist tile on your LogicalCHOICE course screen for reference information and job aids on How to Attach a Macro to an Event

Macros in Access Web Apps

Programmability in Access web apps is provided by a custom macro language authored in the Access client. There are two kinds of macros: user interface macros and data macros. User interface macros can perform actions that affect the user interface of your app, and data macros can work directly with the records contained within the app.

Access Web Apps User Interface Macros

User interface macros let you perform actions such as opening another view, applying a filter, or creating a new record. Embedded user interface macros are attached directly to user interface objects such as command buttons, combo boxes, or the **Action Bar** button object, whereas standalone user interface macros are contained in macro objects.

This table lists the events that you can attach a user interface macro to in a control or view.

Event Type	When It Occurs
After Update	Occurs after you type data into a control or choose data from a control.
On Click	Occurs when a control is selected.
On Current	Occurs when the user moves to a different record in the view.
On Load	Occurs when a view is opened.

This table lists the events supported by each control.

Control or Object Type	Supported Events
Action Bar Button	On Click
AutoComplete	After Update, On Click
Button	On Click
Check Box	After Update
Combo Box	After Update
Hyperlink	After Update, On Click
Image	On Click
Label	On Click
Multiline Textbox	After Update, On Click
Text Box	After Update, On Click
View	On Current, On Load

Access Web Apps Data Macros

Data macros provide a method for implementing business rules at the data layer. Unlike user interface macros, data macros can create, edit, and delete records. Embedded data macros are attached to a table event. Standalone data macros are contained in macro objects.

This table lists the events that you can attach a data macro to in a table.

Event Type	When It Occurs
On Insert	Occurs after a new record is added to the table.
On Update	Occurs after an existing record is changed.
On Delete	Occurs after a record is deleted.

ACTIVITY 3-1
Creating a Macro to Open a New Record on a Form

Data Files

C:\091006Data\Using Macros to Improve User Interface Design\Inventory Database.accdb

Scenario

Users are having difficulty creating a new record in the Inventory form. They don't know about the **New Record** button near the bottom of the screen, so the Data Entry Manager wants you to create a macro that opens the Inventory form, **fmrInventory**, ready to accept a new record.

1. Create a macro for the **frmInventory** form to create a new blank record.
   a) Open **C:\091006Data\Using Macros to Improve User Interface Design\Inventory Database.accdb**. If a security prompt is shown, select **Enable Content**.
   b) Save the file as *My Inventory Database.accdb* and select **Enable Content** if you are prompted.
   c) Select **CREATE→Macros & Code→Macro**.
   d) In the **Add New Action** drop-down list, select the action **OpenForm**.

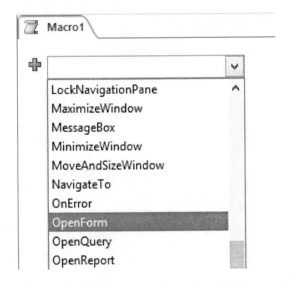

   e) In the **Form Name** drop-down list, select **frmInventory**.
   f) Verify that the **View** drop-down list is set to **Form**.
   g) In the **Data Mode** drop-down list, select **Edit**.
   h) Verify that the **Window Mode** drop-down list is set to **Normal**.

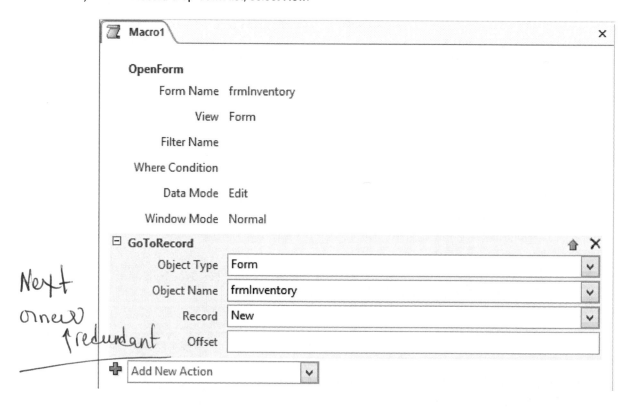

Called Arguments Some mandatory Some n't

Add

xxxX

i) In the **Add New Action** drop-down list, select **GoToRecord**.
j) In the **GoToRecord** action, in the **Object Type** drop-down list, select **Form**.
k) In the **Object Name** drop-down list, select **frmInventory**.
l) In the **Record** drop-down list, select **New**.

Next one) redundant

2. Save and test the macro.

> **Note:** When you save standalone macros, they appear in the newly created **Macro** group in the **All Access Objects** Navigation pane with other objects such as forms, reports, queries, and tables.

a) Save the macro as *mcrInventoryNew*
b) Select **MACRO TOOLS→DESIGN→Tools→Run** to test the macro. It should create a new blank record.

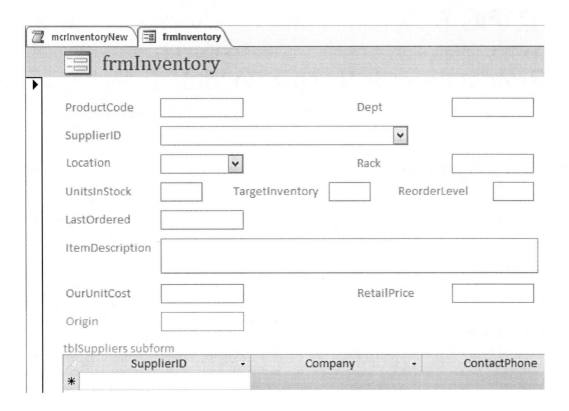

c) Close the form and the macro.

TOPIC B

Restrict Records Using a Condition

In the previous topic, you learned about actions and arguments, so now it's time to look at conditions.

Macro Conditions

A macro *condition* is an expression that enables a macro to perform a task if a specific set of circumstances exist. The macro looks for True/False conditions to take an action. If a condition is True, then the macro takes an action. If False, the macro takes a different action. A single condition can control more than one action.

For example, if you receive orders from customers by phone and you have a particular customer that's behind in payment, then you would like to know that without having to search through records. As soon as you enter the customer name, you want a warning to appear that tells you that this account is frozen until a payment is made. This is a very good example of how a macro could work based on conditions.

If one of your tables includes a column that contains Accounts Payable information and your customer's status show >90 (more than 90 days without payment), then you could create a MessageBox that appears when that customer's account is activated with an order in progress.

Conditions

Conditions are usually the result of an If statement. If this condition exists, then perform some action based on that condition. If the condition does not exist, then either take no action or take a different action. Conditions can be further qualified with a Where condition to filter results.

The Where Condition

The Where condition filters and selects records in forms and reports. You use the Where condition in the OpenForm and OpenReport macro actions. The Where condition can be entered manually or built using the **Expression Builder**.

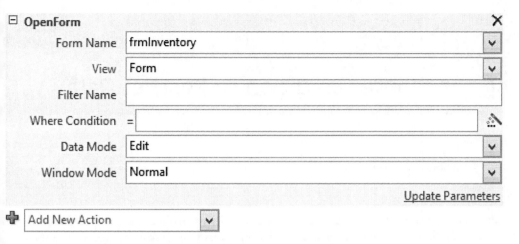

Figure 3-4: The OpenForm macro action with Where Condition.

 Access the Checklist tile on your LogicalCHOICE course screen for reference information and job aids on How to Use a Where Condition in a Macro

ACTIVITY 3-2
Using the Where Condition to Restrict Data

Before You Begin

My Inventory Database.accdb is open.

Scenario

Your manager wants to be able to quickly view all Inventory items that are running low (fewer than nine items in stock). You determine that a good solution for this request is to create a macro that filters the records in the frmInventory form.

---

1. Create a macro that opens frmInventory.
   a) Select **CREATE→Macros & Code→Macro**.
   b) In the **Add New Action** drop-down list, select **OpenForm**.
   c) In the **Form Name** drop-down list, select **frmInventory**.

2. Use the **Expression Builder** to set the condition to alert the user if stock is at or below nine units.

   a) To the right of the **Where Condition** field, select the **Click to invoke Builder** button.
   b) In the **Expression Builder**, in the **Expression Elements** pane, expand **My Inventory Database.accdb**.
   c) Expand **Tables** to view all of the tables in the database.
   d) Select **tblInventory**.

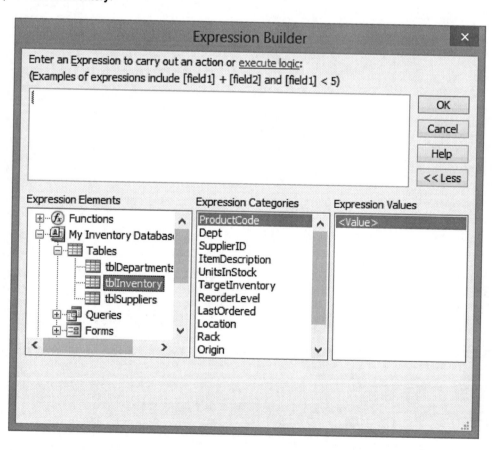

e) In the **Expression Categories** pane, double-click **UnitsInStock**.

f) In the **Enter an expression to carry out an action or execute logic** text box, at the end of the expression that was built with your selections, type *<=9* and then select **OK**.

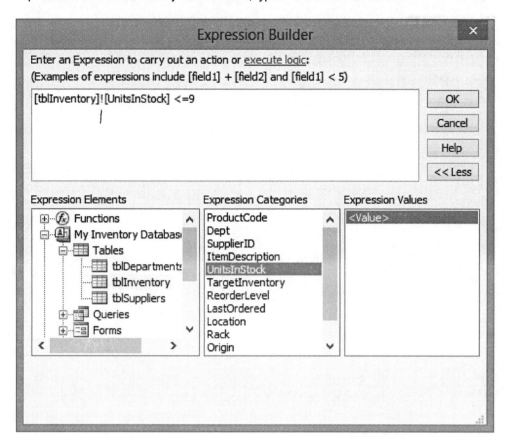

3. Save and test the macro.

   a) Save the macro as *mcrInventoryCheck*

   b) Run the macro.

   c) Verify that the macro displayed the **frmInventory** form and shows 14 records that met the conditions set in the macro.

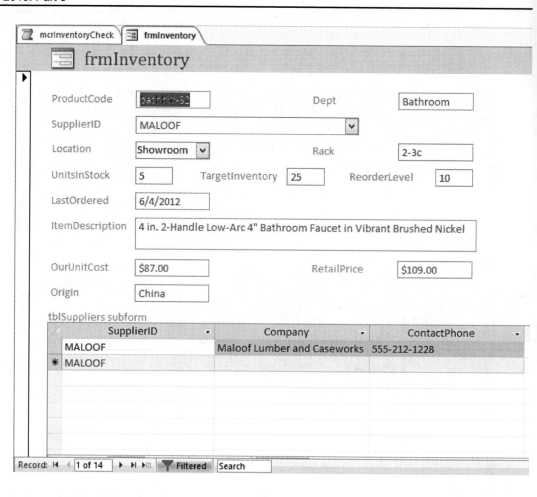

d) Close the form and the macro.

TOPIC C

Validate Data Using a Macro

As previously discussed, data integrity is extremely important. Without accurate data, your database loses value and has to be cleaned up, which consumes time and is quite costly. Creating a macro to prompt the user to enter correct information ensures data integrity and maintains your database's value.

Event Properties for Data Validation

There are four common event properties used to trigger *data validation*.

Event Property	When Execution Will Occur
Before Update	Before the entered data is updated.
After Update	After the entered data is updated.
Before Insert	After a new record is typed in.
On Delete	On delete request, but before deletion.

Macro Actions for Data Validation

When validating data, macros are likely to use certain actions. The following table lists macro actions for data validation.

Action	Action Purpose
CancelEvent	Prevents the user from creating a new record unless certain conditions are ✓ met.
GoToControl	Specifies the data insertion point on a form. *Location*
MessageBox	Displays a custom message to the user.

Embedded Macros

Embedded macros are macros that are part of an event property. They are not standalone database objects. They can only be accessed from the event property of the object they are attached to. You can embed macros in event properties of forms, reports, and controls.

Access the Checklist tile on your LogicalCHOICE course screen for reference information and job aids on How to Use a Macro to Validate Data

ACTIVITY 3-3
Using a Macro to Validate Data

Before You Begin
My Inventory Database.accdb is open.

Scenario
Your manager is happy with your progress on the My Inventory database, but there are still a lot of informational fields that are being left blank when data entry clerks get in a hurry. Your manager wants to ensure that the **SupplierID** field isn't left blank. Each supplier must have an ID before the record is saved. You decide that implementing a macro will help validate this field.

---

1. Open the Macro Builder to begin creating a macro for the **SupplierID** field that runs **On Exit**.
   a) Open the **frmInventory** form in **Design** View.
   b) In the **frmInventory** form, select **SupplierID**.
   c) Display the **Property Sheet** pane.
   d) In the **Property Sheet** pane, select the **Event** tab.
   e) In the **On Exit** field, select the **Choose Builder** button.

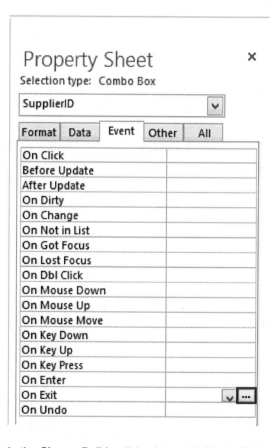

   f) In the **Choose Builder** dialog box, with **Macro Builder** selected, select **OK**.

2. Create a macro to test whether a supplier has been selected.

---

a) In the **Add New Action** drop-down list, select **If**.
b) In the **If** field, type *IsNull([SupplierID])=True*

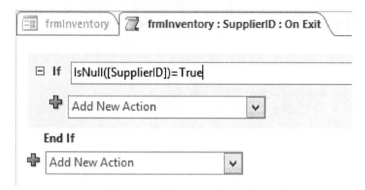

 Note: The IntelliSense feature will try to fill in the options as you type. Do not allow the IntelliSense feature to alter what you are entering.

3. Create a custom message to display if the user doesn't select a supplier.
   a) From within the **If** statement, in the **Add New Action** drop-down list, select **CancelEvent**.

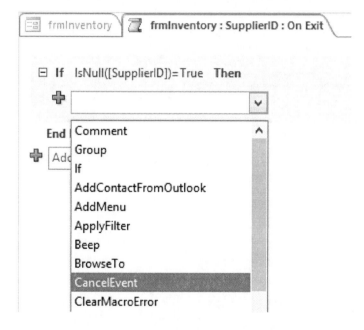

   b) From the **Add New Action** drop-down list within the **If** statement, select **MessageBox**.
   c) In the **MessageBox** action, in the **Message** box, type *You must select a Supplier ID from the list*

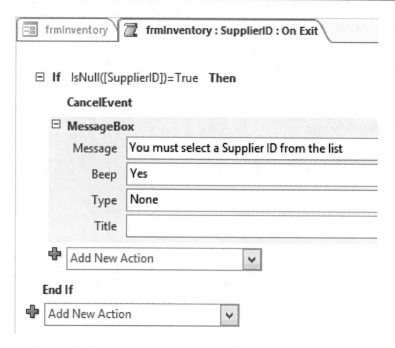

4. Add actions to the macro to force the user to select a supplier.
   a) From the **Add New Action** drop-down list within the **If** statement, select **GoToControl**.
   b) In the **GoToControl** action, in the **ControlName** field, type *SupplierID*

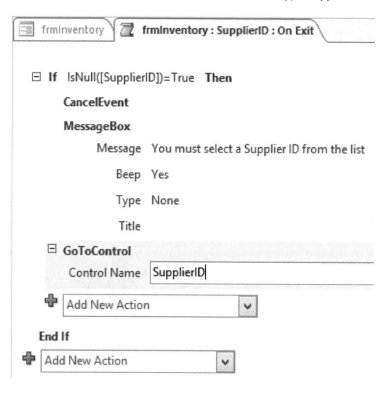

5. Save and test the macro.
   a) Save and close the macro.
   b) Verify that **Embedded Macro** is now listed for the **On Exit** property.

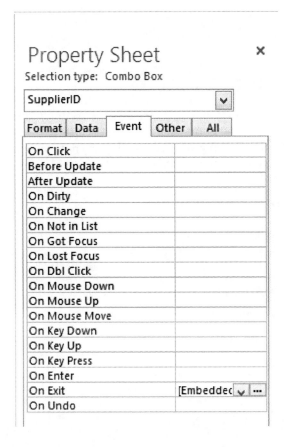

c) Save the form.
d) Display the **frmInventory** in **Form** view.
e) Start a new record.
f) In the new record, in the **Product Code** field, type *bathhw-90* then press **Tab** to move through the rest of the fields.
g) When you attempt to press **Tab** to move past the **SupplierID** field, you should receive the message you created in the macro. Select **OK**.

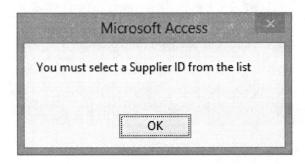

h) Select any supplier from the list, and finish creating the new record and save it.

TOPIC D

Automate Data Entry Using a Macro

Making data entry easy for your users through automation not only increases the accuracy of your data, but also increases the speed at which your users can enter data. For example, if you have your users enter part numbers, the price can be automatically entered based on the part number. You can employ macros to do this work for you by associating them with events.

Event Properties for Automating Data Entry

The event property determines when the event launches the macro.

Event Property	Execution Timing
On Enter	At arrival time onto the control, when the user tabs into the field.
Before Update	Before control data is updated.
After Update	After control data is updated.
On Exit	Upon leaving a control, when the user tabs away from the field.

 Note: For validating data in data entry forms, it is often best to use the **On Exit** event so that when the user tabs away from the field, they receive immediate feedback if their entry is incorrect.

Macro Actions for Automating Data Entry

Macro actions set values and locations for values on forms for automated data entry.

Action	Usage
SetValue	Automatically enter a value into a field. Field name and data value are entered as arguments for **SetValue**.
GoToControl	An action that moves the cursor to the field for data entry.

 Access the Checklist tile on your LogicalCHOICE course screen for reference information and job aids on How to Automate Data Entry with a Macro

Choice Access Key Information

Access keys must be redeemed within 12 months of purchase. Once redeemed, your subscription has no term limit.

Redemption Instructions for **NEW STUDENTS**
To redeem each Access Key, please follow these instructions:
1) Open your Internet Browser (recommended browsers are Firefox, Chrome and Safari):
2) Type in the following URL: http://www.lo-choice.com and press the enter key. This will take you to the login page.
3) Under the "New User" section, enter in your Access Key and click on the "ENROLL" button.
   NOTE: Access Keys are case sensitive. Each Access Key can only be redeemed once.
4) Please fill in all required fields within the Enrollment form. Your Username and Password (Password is at least 6 characters with one being a number) choices are case sensitive in future logins.
5) After completing the enrollment form, you will return to the LO-CHOICE homepage.
6) At the LO-CHOICE homepage, log in under RETURNING USER with your newly created Username and Password.
7) Upon logging in, you will be presented with the LO-CHOICE "Course Screen", which will list the course your access key provided access to. Click the course tile for your course to gain access to the electronic components for your course.

Redemption Instructions for **RETURNING STUDENTS**
To redeem each Access Key, please follow these instructions:
1) Open your Internet Browser (recommended browsers are Firefox, Chrome and Safari):
2) Type in the following URL: http://www.lo-choice.com and press the enter key. This will take you to the login page.
3) Log in under RETURNING USER with your Username and Password.
4) Click on "Add a Course" tile.
5) Enter your Access Key in the pop up window and click "ENROLL". You will now be presented with the LO-CHOICE "Course Screen", which will list the course your access key provided access to, along with all other courses you've redeemed on your account previously. Click the appropriate course tile to gain access to the electronic components for your course.

LogicalCHOICE is available to you 24/7 at http://www.lo-choice.com for the term length of your subscription.

Pif Spray

ACTIVITY 3-4
Automating Data Entry with a Macro

Before You Begin
My Inventory Database.accdb is open, and the **frmInventory** form is displayed in **Form** view.

Scenario
Your manager wants a further tweak of the data entry system to streamline some of the operations and to ease the number of data points users have to enter manually. She wants you to have the database automatically set a value for the Department (Dept) as "Bathroom" for each item that has a product code that begins with "bathhw."

---

1. Open the Macro Builder to begin creating a macro for the **ProductCode** field that runs **On Exit**.
   a) Switch the **frmInventory** form to **Design** view.
   b) Select the **ProductCode** field, and make sure that the **Property Sheet** is visible.
   c) In the **Property Sheet**, in the **On Exit** field, select the **Choose Builder** button.
   d) In the **Choose Builder** dialog box, with **Macro Builder** selected, select **OK**.
   e) In the **Add New Action** drop-down list, select **If**.
   f) In the **If** field, type *[ProductCode] Like "[bathhw]*"*
   g) Select **DESIGN→Show/Hide→Show All Actions**.

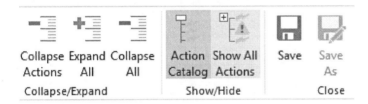

   h) From within the **If** statement, in the **Add New Action** drop-down list, select **SetValue**.
   i) In the **Item** box, type *[Dept]*
   j) In the **Expression** box, type *"Bathroom"*

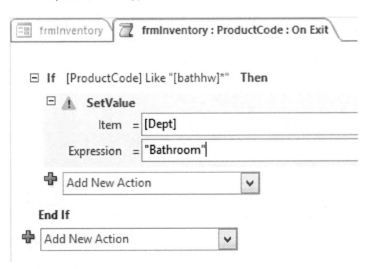

Make sure to include the quotation marks when typing the value.

2. Save and test the macro and the form.
   a) Save and close the macro.
   b) Save the form.
   c) Switch to **Form View** and press **Tab** to deselect **ProductCode**.
   d) Create a new record.
   e) In the **ProductCode** field, type *bathhw-95* and press **Tab**.
   f) Observe that the **Dept** field was automatically populated with the value of **Bathroom**.
   g) Press **Tab**, and select a value in the **SupplierID** drop-down list.

3. Save the record and close the form.

TOPIC E

Convert a Macro to VBA

As you learn to use macros in Access, you will also want to know how to convert a macro to VBA format.

Macros and VBA

To view the code for a macro, the only programmatic element of your databases thus far, you must first convert the macro to Visual Basic for Applications (VBA) code. VBA is a subset of Visual Basic and is used by Microsoft Office applications for scripting inside those applications. One of the main different between VBA and Visual Basic is that VBA cannot compile your project into an executable binary. It will always need a host (Access, Word, or another Office application) to contain and execute the project. Visual Basic for Applications is the preferred procedural language for all of the Microsoft Office products. But, for simplicity, you can continue to use macros and then convert the macro code to VBA.

 Access the Checklist tile on your LogicalCHOICE course screen for reference information and job aids on How to Convert a Macro to VBA

ACTIVITY 3-5
Converting a Macro to VBA

Before You Begin

My Inventory Database.accdb is open.

Scenario

You realize that macros are very handy but are not 100-percent efficient. Additionally, you have some functionality that you would like to implement that might be better handled by a developer using code. You decide to convert your macros to VBA code so that another developer can work with the code and try to optimize it and add more complex logic.

1. Convert the **mcrInventoryCheck** macro to VBA code.
    a) In the **Navigation** pane, under **Macros**, open the **mcrInventoryCheck** macro in **Design** view.
    b) Select **MACRO TOOLS→DESIGN→Tools→Convert Macros to Visual Basic**.
    c) In the **Convert macro: mcrInventoryCheck** dialog box, select **Convert**.

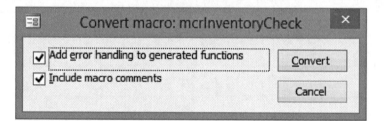

Note: Use the default selections.

d) In the **Convert Macros to Visual Basic** dialog box, select **OK**.

2. View the converted VBA code and close the macro.
    a) In the **Microsoft Visual Basic for Applications** window, select **View→Code**.
    b) Observe the VBA code for the macro.

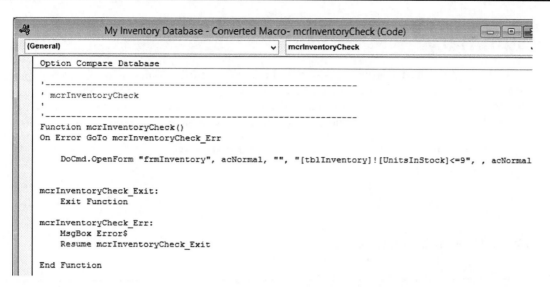

```
My Inventory Database - Converted Macro- mcrInventoryCheck (Code)

(General)                                    mcrInventoryCheck

   Option Compare Database

   '-------------------------------------------------------------
   ' mcrInventoryCheck
   '
   '-------------------------------------------------------------
   Function mcrInventoryCheck()
   On Error GoTo mcrInventoryCheck_Err

       DoCmd.OpenForm "frmInventory", acNormal, "", "[tblInventory]![UnitsInStock]<=9", , acNormal


   mcrInventoryCheck_Exit:
       Exit Function

   mcrInventoryCheck_Err:
       MsgBox Error$
       Resume mcrInventoryCheck_Exit

   End Function
```

   c) Close the **Microsoft Visual Basic for Applications** window to return to the database.

   d) Close the **mcrInventoryCheck** macro.

3. Close the **My Inventory Database** database.

Summary

In this lesson, you used macros to assist users in their data entry. You created a macro to open a new record in a form. You used a macro to display records that met a specific criteria. You also validated whether a user entered required data and automatically filled in a field based on data entered in a different field. All of these macros help users enter data more easily and accurately.

Why would you use a standalone macro versus an embedded macro?

Why would you use a Where condition?

 Note: Check your LogicalCHOICE Course screen for opportunities to interact with your classmates, peers, and the larger LogicalCHOICE online community about the topics covered in this course or other topics you are interested in. From the Course screen you can also access available resources for a more continuous learning experience.

4 Using Advanced Database Management

Lesson Time: 1 hour

Lesson Objectives

In this lesson, you will organize data into appropriate tables to ensure data dependency and minimize redundancy. You will:

- Link tables to external data sources.

- Manage a database.

- Determine object dependency.

- Use **Database Documenter** to document your database.

- Analyze database performance.

Lesson Introduction

Creating tables, queries, forms, reports, and macros is only part of the job of managing a database or multiple databases. As a database designer and administrator, you must perform many non-creative, non-design tasks such as linking your databases to external data sources, managing the links to those external data sources, performing database backups, performing compact and repair on your databases, determining object dependency, database documentation, and analyzing database performance. As the database administrator, you have the responsibility of guaranteeing database integrity through good design, clean data, and a healthy database. This lesson guides you through those processes.

TOPIC A

Link Tables to External Data Sources

Access includes a feature that allows you to link your tables to external data sources. One major advantage of this capability is that when those external files are updated, Microsoft® Access® automatically sees the updates without intervention. This removes responsibility for third-party data from the local Access administrator and from its users. It also expands the possibilities for accessing third-party data that would consume valuable data entry time and valuable space within the Access database.

External Data Sources

Linking your Access tables to *external data sources* might seem esoteric at first, but it is a very important and advanced function. One of the most popular external data sources is an Microsoft® Excel® spreadsheet. Excel spreadsheet use is frequent in companies; therefore, it makes sense for Microsoft to allow Access database designers to connect to these ubiquitous entities as an external source of data.

Excel isn't the only choice for external data sources. You may also attach to other external sources, including other Access databases, SharePoint lists, delimited or fixed-width text files, ODBC databases, HTML documents, Outlook folders, dBASE files, and Paradox files.

The Linked Table Manager

The Linked Table Manager is a utility that refreshes your link to external data. This functionality is useful if an external data source has been updated. The Linked Table Manager displays a list of all linked tables, and you can select the ones you wish to refresh.

 Access the Checklist tile on your LogicalCHOICE course screen for reference information and job aids on How to Use an External Data Source

ACTIVITY 4-1
Using an External Data Source

Data Files

C:\091006Data\Using Advanced Database Management\Inventory Database.accdb

C:\091006Data\Using Advanced Database Management\Faucets.xlsx

Scenario

One of your bathroom faucet suppliers created an Excel spreadsheet catalog for its new line of faucets. They want to supply their retailers with this new catalog. Your manager requests that you use the catalog in your database. You decide that it would be more efficient to use the spreadsheet as an external data source rather than import the data into a table, since suppliers often change their offerings on a seasonal basis.

1. Open the **Inventory Database.accdb**.
   a) Open the **C:\091006Data\Using Advanced Database Management\Inventory Database.accdb**. If a security prompt is shown, select **Enable Content**.
   b) Save the file as *My Inventory Database.accdb*, and select **Enable Content** if you are prompted.

2. Link the database to the Excel spreadsheet **Faucets.xlsx**.
   a) Select **EXTERNAL DATA→Import & Link→Excel**.

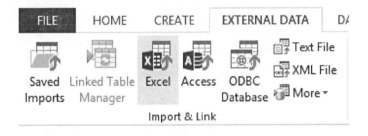

   b) In the **Get External Data - Excel Spreadsheet** dialog box, select **Browse**.
   c) Navigate to **C:\091006Data\Using Advanced Database Management**, select **Faucets.xlsx** and then select **Open**.
   d) Select **Link to the data source by creating a linked table**.
   e) Select **OK**.
   f) In the **Link Spreadsheet Wizard**, select **Sheet1** and then select **Next**.
   g) Check **First Row Contains Column Headings** and then select **Next**.
   h) Name the linked table *tblFaucets* and then select **Finish**.
   i) Select **OK** to acknowledge that your linked table has been created.

3. View the contents of the linked table.
   a) In the **Navigation** pane, open **tblFaucets** in **Datasheet** View.
   b) Observe the Excel data that is linked in the **tblFaucets** table and verify that is actually displayed.

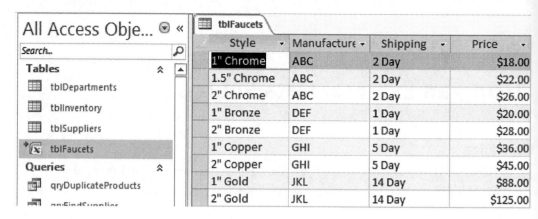

c) Close the **tblFaucets** table.

d) Close the **My Inventory Database** database.

TOPIC B

Manage a Database

A database is a tool and like any other tool, you must perform some regular maintenance and housekeeping on your database to maintain data integrity and overall database health. In this topic, you'll learn two basic Access database management tasks: database backup and how to compact and repair a database.

Exclusive Mode

Any time that you perform actions or maintenance on a database, you need to open it in *exclusive mode*. Exclusive mode means that no one else can access the database but you. This is very important in networked, multi-user databases. Exclusive mode prevents other users from using the database when you are performing maintenance to prevent database or record corruption. When your maintenance is complete, remember to close the database.

Database Access Modes

Access has four basic access modes that you use when opening a database.

Access Mode	Description
Open	Standard or default mode. Multi-user.
Open Read-Only	Cannot write to the database, but can read data.
Exclusive	Only the exclusive user may open the database. Single user.
Exclusive Read-Only	Single user, read-only access.

 Access the Checklist tile on your LogicalCHOICE course screen for reference information and job aids on How to Open a Database in Exclusive Mode

Database Backup

If you've worked with computers for very long, you understand the need for good backups. A backup is a copy of a production database. It is a snapshot of the data and the objects at the time of the backup. Any data entered or any changes made since that backup won't be reflected in the previous backup. This is one reason why database managers perform daily backups. And, the really paranoid database managers perform multiple backups during a day.

There are at least two backup methods for Access databases. One is a simple copy of the database.accdb file to a new location, which is an exact copy of a point in time or snapshot. You create this copy as you would any other file.

The second, preferred method is accomplished through Access itself. Access creates a copy of the current database with a time stamp of your current backup. The backup copy receives its name from the current date. For example, if today's date is December 1, 2012, then your backup for the Inventory Database receives the name, **Inventory Database_2012-12-01.accdb**.

 Access the Checklist tile on your LogicalCHOICE course screen for reference information and job aids on How to Create a Database Backup

The Compact and Repair Database Option

As a database is used, records are inserted, changed, and deleted; tables are ever changing; new forms are being created; reports are generated; and macros are created, edited, and deleted. A database is a dynamic entity. During the course of its use, the database can become fragmented and possibly corrupted. Many of the problems associated with working with databases can be mitigated by performing regular backups and by performing a simple maintenance task known as compact and repair.

The reasons for accidental database corruption are many, but common ones are that during a data entry session, network connectivity is lost to a shared database or there is a problem on the physical disk where the database resides. **Compact and Repair Database** resolves many of these problems by reducing the file size of your database by stitching it back together physically and by checking its file integrity. **Compact and Repair Database** is not a substitute for backups; it is a separate part of maintenance that should be performed on a regular basis. Very busy databases should have **Compact and Repair Database** performed on a daily basis.

If your database is in serious need of maintenance, you might notice status changes on the status bar such as **Removing temporary objects**. However, there are no other prompts or dialog boxes for you to interact with. Everything occurs in the background.

 Access the Checklist tile on your LogicalCHOICE course screen for reference information and job aids on How to Compact and Repair a Database

ACTIVITY 4-2

Compacting and Repairing a Database

Scenario

After taking the Access 2013 course, you realize how important it is to back up and perform a compact and repair database maintenance on your databases. To that end, you decide to perform both on a regular basis.

1. View **My Inventory Database** in exclusive mode.
   a) On the **Welcome** screen, select **Open Other Files**, or select **FILE→Open**.

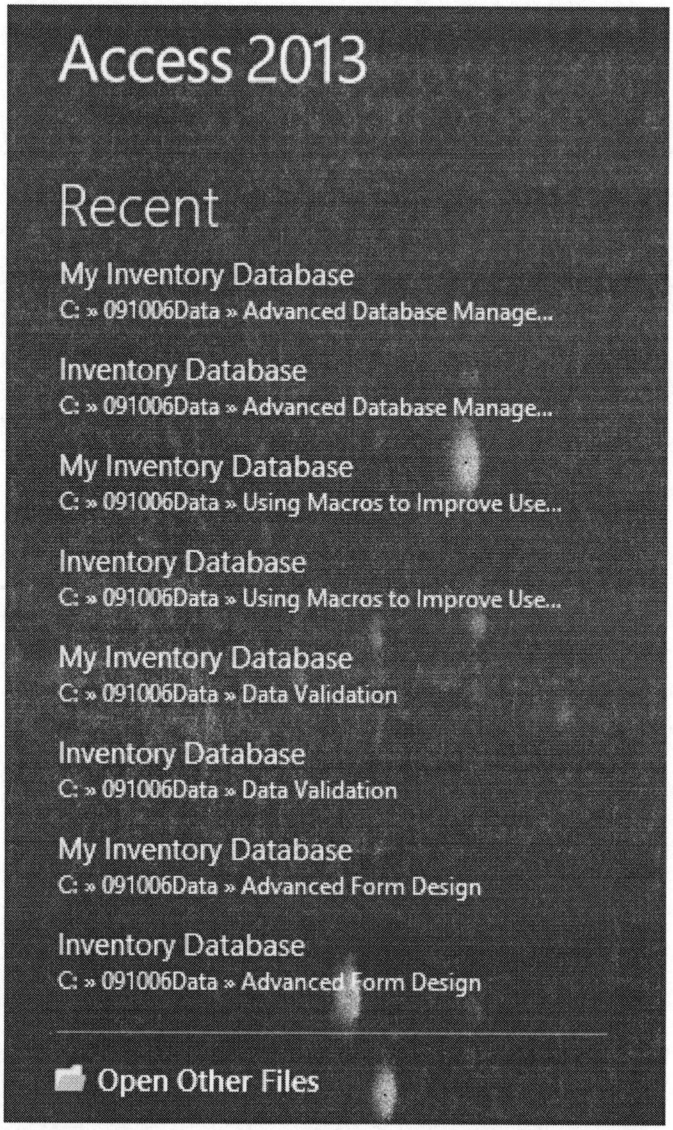

Compact and Repair Claims Hard disk Space.

   b) On the **Open** screen, select **Computer**, and then select **Browse**.
   c) In the **Open** dialog box, navigate to **C:\091006Data\Using Advanced Database Management**.
   d) Select **My Inventory Database**.

e) From the **Open** drop-down list, select **Open Exclusive**.

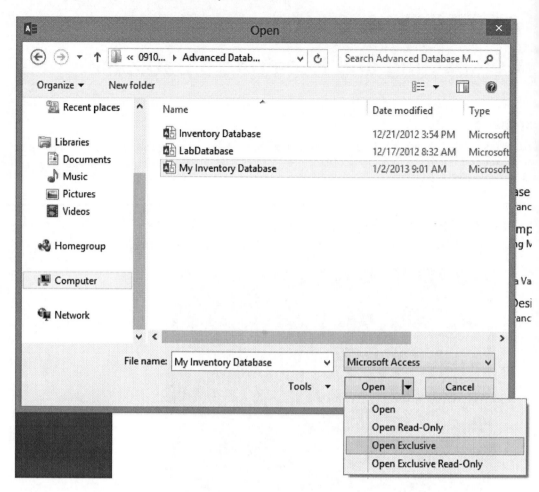

2. Create a backup of **My Inventory Database**.
   a) Select **FILE→Save As**.
   b) On the **Save As** screen, under **Advanced**, select **Back Up Database**.

Save As

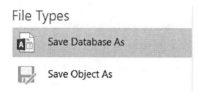

File Types

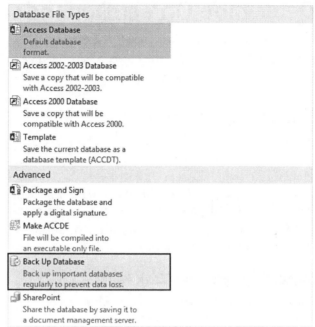

Save Database As

c) Select **Save As**.

d) In the **Save As** dialog box, select **Save**.

3. Compact and repair **My Inventory Database**.

a) Open **Windows Explorer**, and navigate to **C:\091006Data\Using Advanced Database Management**.

b) Record the size of the **My Inventory Database.accdb** file. _____

c) Switch back to **Access**, and select **DATABASE TOOLS→Tools→Compact and Repair Database**.

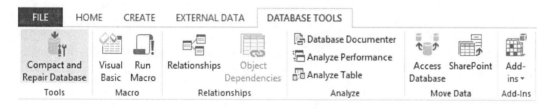

Because this is a relatively small database, the process runs very quickly.

d) Switch to **Windows Explorer** and record the size of the **My Inventory Database.accdb** file.

_____

The file should be smaller now that it has been compacted and repaired.

e) Switch back to Access.

TOPIC C

Determine Object Dependency

All objects in Access have dependencies. Sometimes an object depends on the object you are referring to, and sometimes the object is depended upon by other objects. In this topic, you will examine both types of dependencies.

Object Dependency

Object dependency is when database entities (objects) rely on one another for data. Object dependency in a database can become quite complex, but it's necessary to understand object dependency in cases of advanced troubleshooting. Tables have relationships with each other, and forms have dependencies on queries and on tables. Reports have dependencies on tables, and queries and macros have their dependencies. All database objects can have dependencies.

Access defines two types of dependencies for objects: **Objects that depend on me** and **Objects that I depend on**, where *me* or *I* is the object you select.

Object Dependencies Task Pane

You do not have to open an object to check its dependencies. You can check them through the database tool **Object Dependencies**.

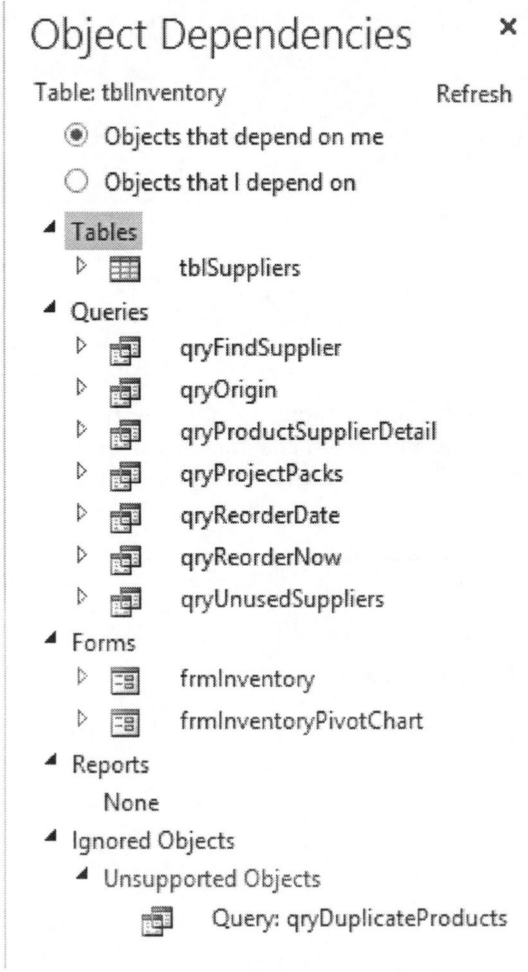

Object Dependencies   ✕

Table: tblInventory   Refresh

- ◉ Objects that depend on me
- ○ Objects that I depend on

▲ **Tables**
  ▷ ⊞ tblSuppliers

▲ Queries
  ▷ 🗃 qryFindSupplier
  ▷ 🗃 qryOrigin
  ▷ 🗃 qryProductSupplierDetail
  ▷ 🗃 qryProjectPacks
  ▷ 🗃 qryReorderDate
  ▷ 🗃 qryReorderNow
  ▷ 🗃 qryUnusedSuppliers

▲ Forms
  ▷ 🖼 frmInventory
  ▷ 🖼 frmInventoryPivotChart

▲ Reports
  None

▲ Ignored Objects
  ▲ Unsupported Objects
      🗃   Query: qryDuplicateProducts

To see what queries

Figure 4-1: The Object Dependencies pane showing Objects that depend on me for tblInventory.

  Access the Checklist tile on your LogicalCHOICE course screen for reference information and job aids on How to Check Object Dependencies

ACTIVITY 4–3
Viewing Object Dependency

Before You Begin

My Inventory Database.accdb is open.

Scenario

One of your users has complained that when she opens the Inventory form, it looks as if the query underlying the **SupplierID** field is coming from another table and feels that something is wrong. You decide to use the **Object Dependencies** task pane to view dependencies and put her mind at ease.

1. View dependencies for **frmInventory**.
   a) In the **Navigation** pane, select, but do not open **frmInventory**.
   b) Select **DATABASE TOOLS→Relationships→Object Dependencies**.

   Notice that no tables depend on this form.
   c) Select **Objects that I depend on**.

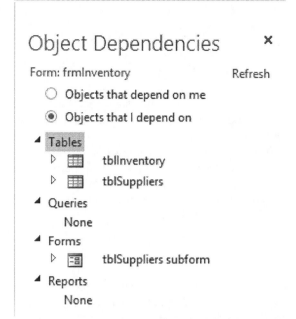

Object Dependencies   ✕

Form: frmInventory   Refresh

   ○ Objects that depend on me

   ◉ Objects that I depend on

◢ Tables
   ▷ ☷   tblInventory
   ▷ ☷   tblSuppliers
◢ Queries
    None
◢ Forms
   ▷ ▣   tblSuppliers subform
◢ Reports
    None

> **Note:** Notice that the form does rely on the **tblSuppliers** and **tblInventory** tables. Why does the form rely on these two tables?

d) Expand **tblInventory** and **tblSuppliers**.

> **Note:** When you expand the **tblInventory** table you see that **tblSuppliers** is listed under it, and when you expand the **tblSuppliers** table you see that **tblInventory** is listed under it. This is because **Object Dependencies** shows the relationships for all of dependencies of the root object. So in this case, **tblInventory** and **tblSuppliers** are both dependencies of **frmInventory**, and they also have a relationship with each other using the **SupplierID** field.

e) Close the **Object Dependencies** pane.

2. Open **frmInventory**, and view the **Property Sheet** to see the relationship to **SupplierID**.

   a) Open **frmInventory** in **Design** view.

   b) Select the **SupplierID** field.

   c) In the **Property Sheet** pane, select the **Data** tab.

   d) Verify that the **Row Source** is the table **tblSuppliers**.

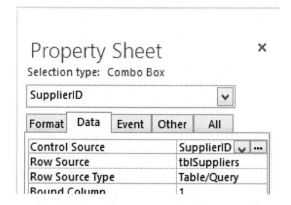

Property Sheet   ✕

Selection type: Combo Box

SupplierID   ⌄

| Format | Data | Event | Other | All |

Control Source	SupplierID ⌄ ⋯
Row Source	tblSuppliers
Row Source Type	Table/Query
Bound Column	1

   e) Close the form.

TOPIC D

Document a Database

You understand what your Inventory database does for you, since you designed it. You understand what all of the embedded macros are for, and you certainly recall all of your validation rules down to the last expression. The problem is that sometimes database designers don't maintain a database throughout its entire life cycle. Those who inherit your masterpiece might not understand the purpose of the validation macro or the other nuances of your work. Therefore, it's necessary to document these items. Documentation isn't as exciting as creating a form that queries inventory information, makes automated updates to fields, and then calculates profit and loss but it's very important. In this topic, you'll use the **Database Documenter** tool.

The Database Documenter

The **Database Documenter** is an automated tool to document every detail of your database schema. This tool, like the Backup tool, is a snapshot in time. If you change one thing in your database, such as adding a form, you need to update the documentation for it.

Access creates very detailed documentation, which can take several minutes to complete if you have a lot of components in the database. When the **Database Documenter** is finished, the documentation is displayed on screen. The documentation is not automatically saved in your database or as an external file. You can save the documentation as a PDF or XPS file.

> Access the Checklist tile on your LogicalCHOICE course screen for reference information and job aids on How to Document a Database with Database Documenter

ACTIVITY 4-4
Using the Database Documenter

Before You Begin
My Inventory Database.accdb is open.

Scenario
You've been promoted to Database Designer at your company and now all of your maintenance, daily housekeeping, and minor changes have been delegated to other employees. Your manager has advised you to prepare the appropriate documentation for all of your databases so that there can be a smooth hand-off and so that you won't be bothered with a lot of questions about functionality and purpose of databases that you've created and maintained. You realize that you have created too many databases for it to be reasonable to go back and create documentation for each one. Fortunately, you remember the **Database Documenter** in Access.

---

1. Create documentation for **My Inventory Database**.
   a) Select **DATABASE TOOLS→Analyze→Database Documenter**.
   b) In the **Documenter** dialog box, select the **All Object Types** tab.

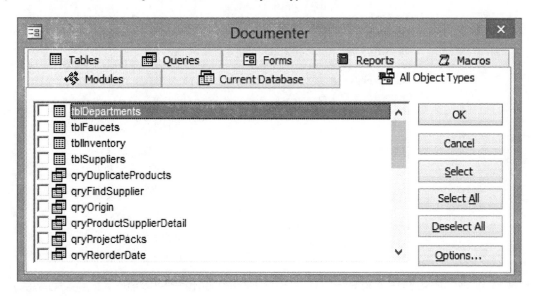

   c) Select **Select All** to select all database objects.
   d) Select **tblInventory**.
   e) Select **Options** to see the documentation details.
   f) Select **OK** to leave the options at their defaults.
   g) Select **OK** to create the documentation.

2. Save the documentation as a PDF file.
   a) Select **PRINT PREVIEW→Zoom→Zoom**.

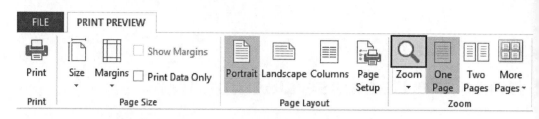

b) Scroll through the report, and observe the documentation.
c) Right-click the documentation and select **Export**, and then select **PDF or XPS**.

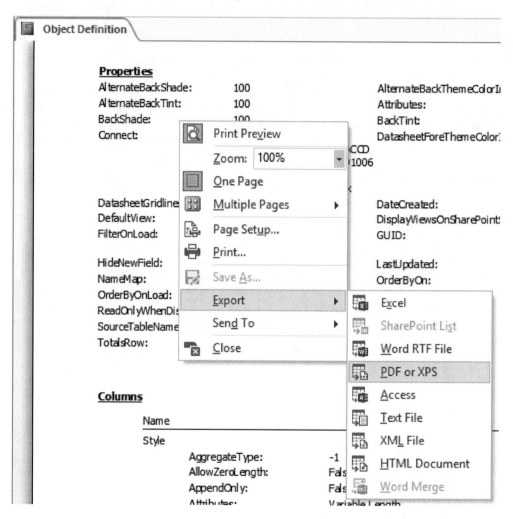

d) In the **Publish as PDF or XPS** dialog box, navigate to C:\091006Data\Using Advanced Database Management.
e) In the **File name** box, type *Inventory Documentation* and then select **Publish** to save the file.

 Note: This may take up to one minute to complete.

f) If necessary, switch back to **Access**, and in the **Export - PDF** dialog box, select **Save Export Steps**.

 Note: The saved export steps are saved the same location as the exported file.

g) Select **Save Export**.
h) Close the **Object Definition** documentation and **Inventory Documentation.pdf**.

TOPIC E

Analyze the Performance of a Database

One of the things you never want to hear your users say is, "The database is slow." First, because that information doesn't help you pinpoint a problem. Second, because there's a problem somewhere, and you have to locate it and fix it. Just as regular backups can prevent disasters and regular compact and repair can prevent corruption, performance analysis can help you identify and fix problems before you get those dreaded calls about database slowness. Access has a built-in tool, the **Performance Analyzer**, that's designed to help you do just that: analyze performance.

Performance Analyzer

More than the basic function of analyzing performance, the Access **Performance Analyzer** tool also recommends improvements to you.

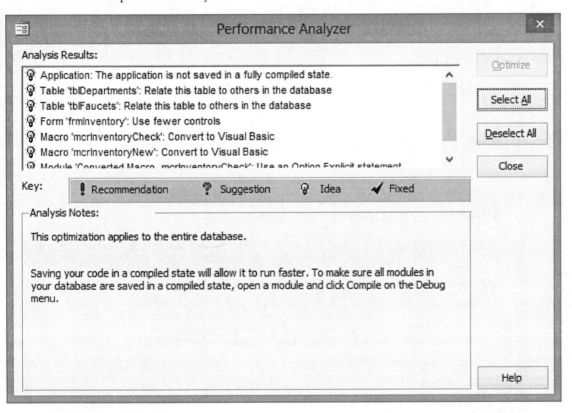

Figure 4-2: Analysis results.

Access the Checklist tile on your LogicalCHOICE course screen for reference information and job aids on How to Use Performance Analyzer

ACTIVITY 4–5
Using the Performance Analyzer

Before You Begin

My Inventory Database.accdb is open.

Scenario

Your manager overheard two of the data entry clerks discussing how they think something might be wrong with My Inventory Database because, as they put it, "It's getting slow." Your manager has asked you to stay after work and to see if you can do anything to speed it up.

1. Analyze the performance of **My Inventory Database**.
   a) Select **DATABASE TOOLS→Analyze→Analyze Performance**.

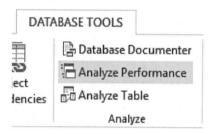

   b) In the **Performance Analyzer** dialog box, select the **All Object Types** tab.
   c) Select **Select All** to select all of the database objects for analysis.

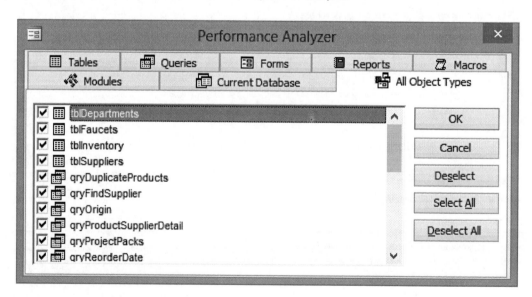

   d) Select **OK** to begin the analysis.

2. Review the analysis.
   a) Read the recommendations, ideas, and suggestions.
   b) Select one of the results and review the **Analysis Notes** for the selected item.

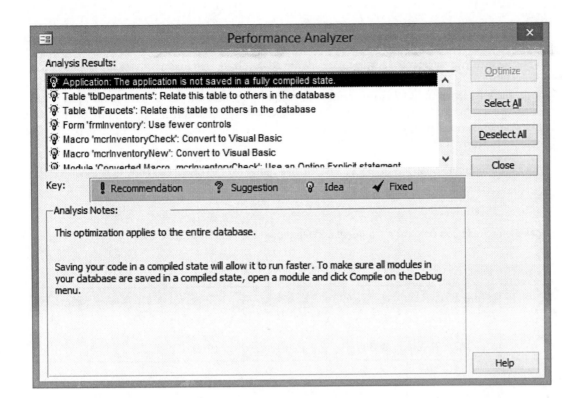

	Note: The results don't necessarily indicate any serious problems. Those may exists but many of these suggestions are focused on optimizing the database for performance.

c) Select **Close**.

d) Close the database.

Summary

In this lesson, you performed a variety of advanced database management tasks. You started by linking tables to external data sources. Next, you managed databases by opening them in exclusive mode, backing them up, and compacting and repairing them. Next, you examined object dependencies, both objects that depend on the selected object and those objects that the selected object depends on. Then, you used the built-in tool to document a database. Finally, you analyzed database performance.

Why it is important to open the database in exclusive mode prior to performing any maintenance?

How often should you perform a Compact and Repair on the databases you use?

 Note: Check your LogicalCHOICE Course screen for opportunities to interact with your classmates, peers, and the larger LogicalCHOICE online community about the topics covered in this course or other topics you are interested in. From the Course screen you can also access available resources for a more continuous learning experience.

5 Distributing and Securing a Database

Lesson Time: 1 hour, 10 minutes

Lesson Objectives

In this lesson, you will lock down and prepare a database for distribution to multiple users. You will:

- Prepare a database for multiple user access.

- Implement security.

- Set a database password.

- Convert an Access database to an ACCDE database.

- Package a database with a digital signature.

Lesson Introduction

Microsoft® Access® provides database administrators with tools to move from a single user database to a multi-user networked database application. Microsoft has done a great job in leveraging Access to do a lot of heavy database application work before moving up to Microsoft's SQL Server®. And, if you need to move up to SQL Server, Microsoft Access allows you to do so seamlessly. This lesson guides you in preparing your database for multi-user access by splitting your databases into front-end and back-end components. You're also given tools to implement security for your databases, including trusted locations, passwords, conversion to ACCDE format, and digital signatures.

TOPIC A

Split a Database for Multiple User Access

The purpose of a database is to store and consume information. Databases can remain private or single user, but many users can also use them. Multi-user databases sometimes encounter performance problems over time. You learned in the previous lesson that you can analyze performance and make changes to enhance your overall database experience. This topic introduces you to a method of increasing database performance for multi-user access: splitting the database. Performance isn't the only reason why database administrators split Access databases but it certainly tops the list of reasons.

Splitting a Database

Splitting a database is a simple process that divides your single ACCDB file into two files. One file becomes the font-end database and contains the presentation components consisting of forms, queries, reports, and macros. The second file becomes the back-end database and contains the data in tables. In multi-user environments, this reduces network traffic and allows continuous front-end development without affecting data or interrupting users.

You don't have to do anything special when opening a database that has been split. Open the ACCDB file as usual and your tables will be there. Essentially, what the database splitter does is move your tables to a separate database and then attaches the tables as external data sources like those covered in the topic *Linking Tables to External Data Sources*. You can see this by examining the tables in your split database. Note the external data link symbol associated with them. Compare it to the **tblFaucets** table as shown in the following figure.

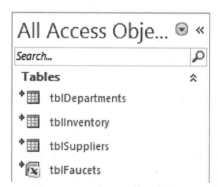

Figure 5-1: Viewing tables in a split database.

Front-end and Back-end Databases

For discussions of these two files, the one that contains the presentation components is the front-end database file with the standard ACCDB name, My Inventory Database.accdb, for example. The second file (containing the tables) uses the file name ACCDB_BE to designate it as the back-end database.

The Database Splitter

The **Database Splitter** is the tool that splits your database into the two parts. It's a very simple process to perform. You will need to open the database in exclusive mode prior to splitting the database. Once your database is split into the ACCDB and the ACCDB_BE files, you can open the back-end database to see for yourself that it only contains tables.

 Access the Checklist tile on your LogicalCHOICE course screen for reference information and job aids on How to Split a Database

ACTIVITY 5–1
Splitting a Database

Data Files

C:\091006Data\Distributing and Securing a Database\Inventory Database.accdb

Scenario

You've decided to split your database due to the increased number of over-the-network users in your organization. You have your manager's permission to make the change. You've already made a backup of your database prior to this activity.

---

1. Open the **Inventory Database**.
   a) Open **C:\091006Data\Distributing and Securing a Database\Inventory Database.accdb** in exclusive mode. If a security prompt is shown, select **Enable Content**.
   b) Save the file as *My Inventory Database.accdb*, and select **Enable Content** if you are prompted.

2. Split the database.
   a) Select **DATABASE TOOLS→Move Data→Access Database**.
   b) In the **Database Splitter** dialog box, read the information, and then select **Split Database**.

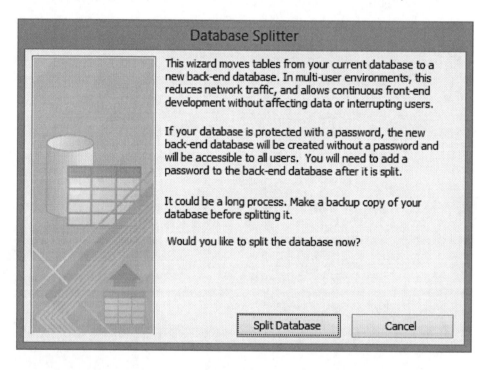

Database Splitter

This wizard moves tables from your current database to a new back-end database. In multi-user environments, this reduces network traffic, and allows continuous front-end development without affecting data or interrupting users.

If your database is protected with a password, the new back-end database will be created without a password and will be accessible to all users. You will need to add a password to the back-end database after it is split.

It could be a long process. Make a backup copy of your database before splitting it.

Would you like to split the database now?

Split Database   Cancel

   c) If not already there, browse to the **C:\091006Data\Distributing and Securing a Database** folder.
   d) Select **Split** to save **My Inventory Database_be.accdb** to the selected folder.
   e) In the informational message box that is displayed stating that your database successfully split, select **OK**.
   f) In the **Navigation** pane, observe the tables listed in the **Tables** section. The arrow to the left of the tables indicates that the table is located in an external database, in this case the **My Inventory Database.accdb_be** file.

 Note: To learn how to normalize the databases you create, see the LearnTO **Normalize a Database** presentation from the **LearnTO** tile on the LogicalCHOICE Course screen.

TOPIC B

Implement Security

It seems that everyone in the computing business is obsessed with security. But, the paranoia is not altogether unfounded. Hardly a day goes by without hearing about some website, bank, or company that's been hacked and had its data security compromised. It's an unfortunate side effect of our technology dependence. Fortunately, Microsoft knows this and provides you with adequate security measures in Access. Of course, no security strategy is 100-percent foolproof. Security is an ongoing battle that, at best, ends in a draw.

In an on-premise environment, Access web apps are hosted by SharePoint 2013, while the data is stored in SQL Server 2012. Because of this, SharePoint 2013 provides authentication, authorization, and security for Access web apps.

Security Strategies in Access 2013

Access 2013 offers several different security strategies.

Strategy	Implementation
Database Password	Encrypt and password protect the database. This is a basic security strategy.
Secure VBA code	Password protect VBA code to prevent copying and editing.
Startup Options	Automatically open a Switchboard or other form. Setting other options to protect parts of the database.
Hide Database Objects	Prevent users from seeing objects in the **Navigation** pane.
Trust Center Options	Set Trusted Locations and options for databases.
Digital Signatures	A signed certificate verifies that the database is from a trusted or reliable source.

The Message Bar

In Access, the Message Bar appears just below the ribbon and displays important security information to the user. The types of messages that appear in the message bar include security alerts, policy messages, workflow tasks, and server information. If the message bar has been hidden, select **FILE→Options→Trust Center→Trust Center Settings→Message Bar**, and then select **Show the Message Bar in all applications when active content, such as ActiveX controls and macros, has been blocked.**

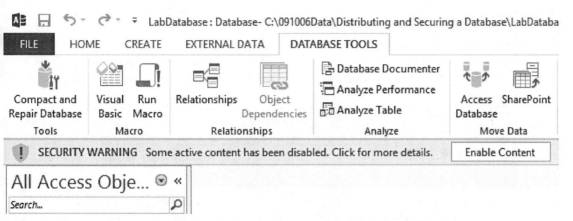

Figure 5-2: The message bar appears to inform users of security information.

The Trust Center Dialog Box

The *Trust Center* dialog box allows you to set security options for Access. The **Trust Center** dialog box options determine how much or how little security is set on your database from a user-experience perspective. That is to say, if you change settings here, your user's experience with database security will change. For example, you can disable the Message Bar notices from appearing, which will never show any messages about blocked content.

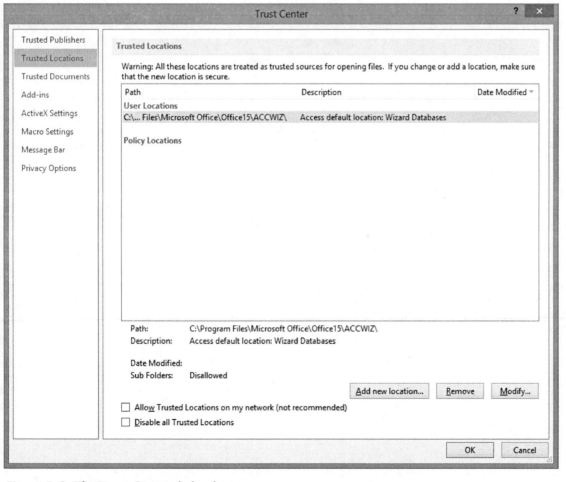

Figure 5-3: The Trust Center dialog box.

Trusted Locations

A *trusted location* is a folder that is known to Microsoft Access as a location that should not be checked by the Trust Center. The purpose of trusted locations is to prevent any warnings about macros, ActiveX controls, or data connections that the Trust Center ordinarily would see as potentially harmful.

 Note: For shared databases, you can designate a shared network folder as a trusted location. Contact your System Administrator to add password security on the folder allowing only authenticated users to use the location.

 Access the Checklist tile on your LogicalCHOICE course screen for reference information and job aids on How to Add a Trusted Location

ACTIVITY 5-2
Adding a Trusted Location

Before You Begin
My Inventory Database.accdb is open.

Scenario
Since you've split your database, you've decided to begin implementing security for your databases. One of those security methods is to place back-end database files into a trusted location on a network drive.

Add a trusted location.
a) Select **FILE→Options**.
b) Select the **Trust Center** tab.
c) Select **Trust Center Settings**.
d) Select **Trusted Locations**.
e) Select **Add New Location**.
f) In the **Path** text box, type *C:\091006Data\Distributing and Securing a Database* for the path for the trusted location.

 Note: The trusted location can be anywhere you choose, but it should be a location that is appropriate for storing the database. If you were really adding a network location, the path would be different.

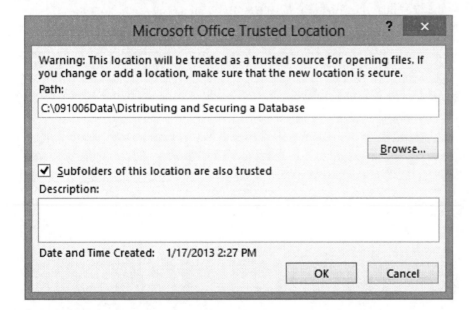

g) Select **Subfolders of this location are also trusted**.
h) Select **OK** three times.

TOPIC C

Set Passwords

Just as you use passwords to access your computer, your network, and other resources, you can use passwords on Access databases. Passwords help you keep your data secure. In this topic, you will set a password on a database.

Password Protection

Setting a password on a database is a first line of defense security measure. However, a password is only one measure that you should take in your total security strategy. Follow standard password rules when assigning passwords to databases. Using a password prevents unauthorized access to a database that might contain sensitive data. It also sends an implied warning message that this database's information is private.

Guideline	Implementation
Length	Use at least eight characters. More characters adds strength.
Numbers	Add at least one numeric character.
Capitalization	Use a mixture of upper and lower case letters.
Alternative characters	Use at least one of these characters: ! @ # $ % ^ & * ( ).
Letter substitution	Be careful to avoid using standard character substitutions such as @ for a, $ for s, and 3 for e.

 Access the Checklist tile on your LogicalCHOICE course screen for reference information and job aids on How to Set a Database Password

ACTIVITY 5-3
Setting a Database Password

Before You Begin
My Inventory Database.accdb is open.

Scenario
Since your database is used by several different departments, some unauthorized, your manager has suggested that you password-protect it so that only authorized users may access it. You already sent users an email letting them know the database will be unavailable during the time you are setting the password.

1. Open **My Inventory Database** in exclusive mode.
   a) Close the **My Inventory Database** database.
   b) Select **FILE→Open**.
   c) On the **Open** screen, select **Computer**, and then select **Browse**.
   d) In the **Open** dialog box, navigate to **C:\091006Data\Distributing and Securing a Database**.
   e) Select **My Inventory Database**.
   f) From the **Open** drop-down list, select **Open Exclusive**.

2. Set a password for the database.
   a) Select **FILE→Info**.
   b) On the **Info** screen, select **Encrypt with Password**.

Info

My Inventory Database
C: » 091006Data » Distributing and Securing a Database

Compact & Repair Database

Compact & Repair
Help prevent and correct database file problems by using Compact and Repair.

Encrypt with Password

Encrypt with Password
Use a password to restrict access to your database. Files that use the 2007 Microsoft Access file format or later are encrypted.

   c) On the **Set Database Password** dialog box, in the **Password** text box, type *Password*
   d) In the **Verify** text box, type *Password* and then select **OK**.
   e) In the message box, select **OK** to acknowledge the message about row level locking.

 Note: Row level locking is one method for locking data when multiple users try to access the same data. By default, Access uses record level locking.

3. Test the password.

a) Close the database.
b) Open the **C:\091006Data\Distributing and Securing a Database\My Inventory Database.accdb** file.
c) When prompted for the password, type *Password* and select **OK**.

TOPIC D

Convert an Access Database to an ACCDE File

If you want to prevent anyone from creating or modifying forms, reports, or code in your Access database, you can convert the database to an Access Execute Only Database, or ACCDE database. Converting the database to the ACCDE file format is another way to secure your database. In this topic, you will convert your database to an ACCDE database.

The ACCDE File Format

The ACCDE file format is an Access database that has been converted from the standard ACCDB file to the Execute Only file type. The ACCDE is a locked-down version of your database. This means that users cannot make design changes to forms, reports, macros, or VBA code. If you're distributing your database to users outside of your design group, then it's wise to convert them first so that you don't have users changing your design elements.

 Note: When you save the ACCDE file and return to your database, you return to the original ACCDB file, not the newly saved ACCDE version.

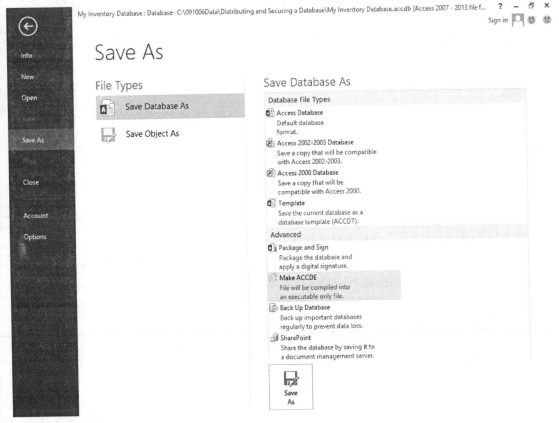

Figure 5–4: Creating an ACCDE file from an open database.

User Templates

For creating entire specific-use databases, Access supplies you with five templates, or Application Parts, from which to choose: **Comments, Contacts, Issues, Tasks,** and **Users.** You'll find these templates on the ribbon under **CREATE→Application Parts→Quick Start.** The tables and forms created by these templates function like any other tables and forms and can be used with queries, reports, and so forth.

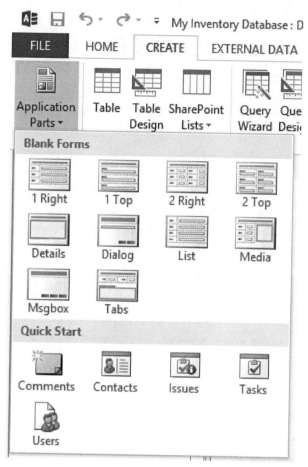

Figure 5–5: The Quick Start Database Templates menu.

The templates provide you with a complete database that may include tables, queries, forms, and reports. The template databases contain no data.

Saving Databases as Templates

You, as a database creator and designer, can also save a database as a template. The file format for an Access database template is ACCDT. ACCDT is another file extension you may see in the backstage along with ACCDE. For example, if you create a payments database as **Payments.accdb**, then you can save that database as *Payments.accdt*. As part of the distribution mechanism for your databases, Access gives you the opportunity to customize your template prior to saving it. Once you've customized your template, using the dialog box shown in the following figure, it will appear in the list with the other templates in the ribbon.

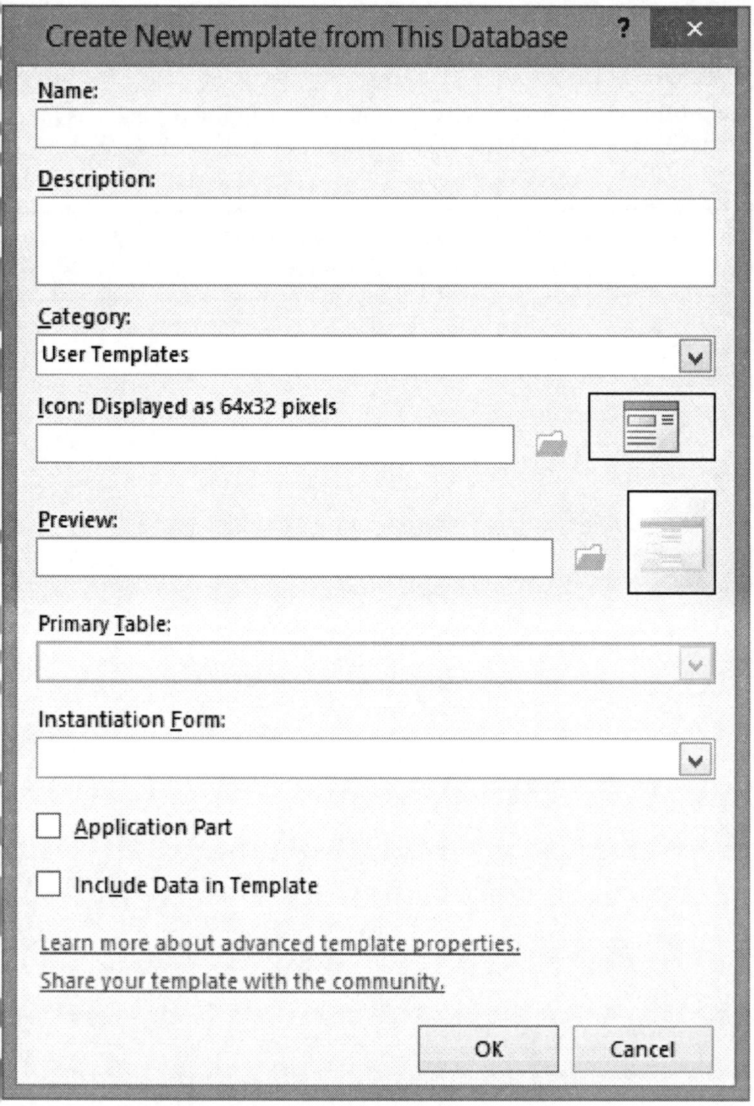

Figure 5-6: Customizing a template for distribution.

The following are the components of the **Create New Template from This Database** dialog box:

*   **Name:** A required field that identifies the template. Access displays this name with the template.
*   **Description:** The purpose of the template. This description appears in the ToolTip for the template.
*   **Category:** Select **User Templates** to have the template show up under **User Templates** on the ribbon. You can also add a category by typing it and you can then assign this and future templates to that category. The new category will show up in the ribbon.
*   **Icon:** You can specify an icon to display for your template.
*   **Preview:** Provide a larger image to display for the template in **Backstage** view. When you browse for a template, this image is what you will see for it.
*   **Primary Table:** Select a table that will be the primary table for the template. When someone uses the template, Access starts a wizard to help create a relationship between this table and others. Although the primary table is used by default, you can select a different table when the wizard runs.
*   **Instantiation Form:** Select a form that will open by default when databases made from this template are first opened.

- **Application Part**: Select this check box to save the database as an Application Part. Clear this check box to save the database as a database template. You must select this check box before you can specify a value for the primary table.
- **Include Data in Template**: Select this check box to save the data that is in the database as part of the template. When new databases are created from the template, they include this data.

 Access the Checklist tile on your LogicalCHOICE course screen for reference information and job aids on How to Convert an Access Database to an ACCDE File

ACTIVITY 5-4
Converting a Database to ACCDE Format

Before You Begin
My Inventory Database.accdb is open in exclusive mode.

Scenario
Upper management has decided that this database needs wider distribution in the company, but an effort needs to be made to avoid structural changes to the database design. They want users to add records but no other changes. You know that if you convert the database to an ACCDE format, it prevents those changes. You have already made a backup of your database.

---

1. Save that database as ACCDE format.
   a) Select **FILE→Save As**.
   b) On the **Save As** screen, select **Make ACCDE**.
   c) Select **Save As**.
   d) Browse to **C:\091006Data\Distributing and Securing a Database**.
   e) Select **Save**.

2. Test the ACCDE database.
   a) Select **FILE→Open**.
   b) On the **Open** page, select **Computer**.
   c) Under **Current Folder**, select **Distributing and Securing a Database**.
   d) In the **Open** dialog box, select **My Inventory Database.ACCDE**, and then select **Open**.

    Note: If file extensions are not visible, then expand the **Type** column, and select the database that has a **Type** of **Microsoft Access ACCDE Database**.

Name	Date modified	Type
Inventory Database	1/11/2013 1:38 PM	Microsoft Access Database
LabDatabase	1/2/2013 1:43 PM	Microsoft Access Database
My Inventory Database	1/17/2013 3:08 PM	Microsoft Access Database
My Inventory Database	1/17/2013 3:10 PM	Microsoft Access ACCDE Database
My Inventory Database_be	1/17/2013 3:10 PM	Microsoft Access Database

   e) If prompted for a password, type *Password* and then select **OK**.
   f) In the **Navigation** pane, open the **frmInventory** form.
   g) Right-click the **frmInventory** tab, and observe that the only view available is the **Form View**.

    Note: Because this database uses the ACCDE format, no design or layout changes can be made to it.

TOPIC E

Package a Database with a Digital Signature

A database contains code in the form of macros, VBA code, and actions that users can be apprehensive about. When you package your database for distribution to users outside of your workgroup or trust zone, you want those users to trust your content, code included, and use your database with confidence. Digitally signing your database with a certificate provides this confidence by informing the user that the content is safe and signed by you as such.

Digital Signatures

A *digital signature* is an authentication tool that verifies the content in a file. It tells the user that the content can be trusted. It's used to validate the source of the content and identify the content as safe to use. A digital signature is used by Access to verify the source of a database against its list of trusted publishers.

Digital Certificates

A *digital certificate* is an identification tool. It verifies the identity of the data creator and sender. The certificate contains the name of the file publisher, the expiration date, a serial number, and a public key. Access 2013 allows you to create a self-signed digital certificate.

The Package and Sign Feature

The Access 2013 Package and Sign feature creates an Access deployment file, which is known as an Access Signed Package. It uses the ACCDC file type to denote that it contains a digital signature. The Package and Sign feature also compresses the database so that it is easily distributed via email or file transfer methods.

 Access the Checklist tile on your LogicalCHOICE course screen for reference information and job aids on How to Digitally Sign a Database

ACTIVITY 5-5
Digitally Sign a Database

Before You Begin

My Inventory Database.accde is open, and frmInventory is displayed in **Form** view.

Scenario

Since you're going to be packaging your database for wider use, you need to assign it a Digital Certificate to guarantee authenticity to those who receive it.

---

1. Create a digital certificate.

    Note: You only have to type as much of the Digital Certificate for VBA Projects as needed to bring it up in the list of programs.

   a) In **Windows 8**, in the **Charm** bar, select **Search**.

   b) In the **Search** text box, type *Digital Certificate for VBA Projects*

   c) On the **Apps** screen, select **Digital Certificate for VBA Projects**.

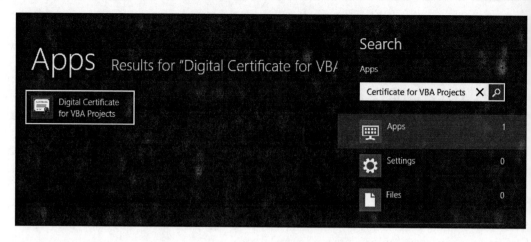

d) In the **Create Digital Certificate** dialog box, in the **Your certificate's name** text box, type *My Inventory Certificate*

e) Select **OK**.

f) On the **SelfCert Success** dialog box, select **OK**.

2. Sign the database with your certificate.

a) Switch back to **Access**.

b) Select **FILE→Save As**.

c) On the **Save As** screen, select **Package and Sign** and then select **Save As**.

d) In the **Windows Security** dialog box, select **My Inventory Certificate** and then select **OK**.

e) Browse to **C:\091006Data\Distributing and Securing a Database** and then select **Create**.
The file is saved with the .accdc file extension, indicating that the file has been signed with a certificate.

f) Close the database.

Note: By digitally signing your database you show that you believe the database is safe and that its content can be trusted by adding a digital signature to the database. If you plan on distributing your database then it helps people who use the database decide whether to trust it and its content.

Summary

In this lesson, you secured your database in several ways. You split the database to create a front-end and a back-end database to ready the database for use by multiple users. You set up a trusted location and added a password to the database. You converted the database to an ACCDE file format so that users cannot change or create forms, reports, or code in your database. Finally, you packaged and digitally signed the database. All of these measures combined help secure the integrity of your database.

Which security measures will you implement for your databases?

Will you be splitting your databases? Why or why not?

 Note: To explore using an Access database as a web database, see the LearnTO **Use Access as a Web Database** presentation from the **LearnTO** tile on the LogicalCHOICE Course screen.

 Note: Check your LogicalCHOICE Course screen for opportunities to interact with your classmates, peers, and the larger LogicalCHOICE online community about the topics covered in this course or other topics you are interested in. From the Course screen you can also access available resources for a more continuous learning experience.

6 | Managing Switchboards

Lesson Time: 30 minutes

Lesson Objectives

In this lesson, you will create and modify a database switchboard and set the startup options. You will:

• Create a switchboard.

• Modify a switchboard.

• Set startup options.

Lesson Introduction

You have seen a variety of methods to make your database more secure and make the database easier for users to use. Now you can limit users to the database objects that they need to use and make it easier for them to access those objects.

TOPIC A

Create a Database Switchboard

Think of your switchboard and its components as you would if you were designing web pages to navigate around your website. The switchboard is similar to the Index page of a website. If you're not familiar with website construction, think of your switchboard as being similar to the Table of Contents in a book. But, instead of page numbers, you have links to forms or buttons that perform some action for you.

Switchboards

In Microsoft® Access®, a *switchboard* is a form that usually opens when you open a database. It is the master form. You can place anything you want on a switchboard: links to other forms, links to reports, and control buttons to close the database, print, or exit Access. You should design your switchboard with the idea that it is the user's primary database interface. Chances are good that you'll hide the other components of your database, so a well-designed switchboard is essential to a smooth user experience.

Switchboard Manager

Before you create a switchboard, you'll have to make the Switchboard Manager visible to you. Once it is visible, it will stay on the ribbon and be available when you need to create or modify a **Switchboard** form. The difference in using the Switchboard Manager and simply creating a form as a switchboard is that you have the advantage of the Switchboard Manager, which is designed specifically to help create a complex form as a switchboard.

The Switchboard Manager Dialog Box

When you first open the Switchboard Manager, you receive a message that the Switchboard Manager was unable to find a valid switchboard in this database and asks if you would like to create one.

Figure 6–1: The initial message from the Switchboard Manager.

After you select **Yes**, the **Switchboard Manager** dialog box opens to assist creation of your switchboard.

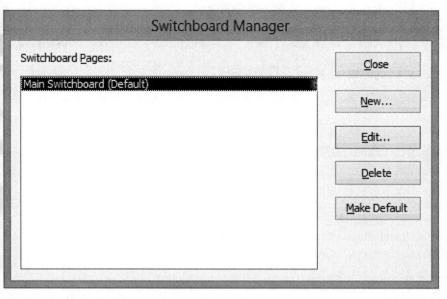

Figure 6-2: The Switchboard Manager dialog box.

 Access the Checklist tile on your LogicalCHOICE course screen for reference information and job aids on **How to Create a Switchboard**

ACTIVITY 6–1
Creating a Simple Switchboard

Data Files

C:\091006Data\Managing Switchboards\Inventory Database.accdb

Scenario

Now that your database is more complex and widely used, users are complaining that it's too difficult to use, and they don't know which item to open for a particular task. You decide to create a simple navigation screen, or switchboard, for your users. First, you have to add the **Switchboard Manager** to your ribbon so that you'll have easy access to it now and in the future.

---

1. Open the **Inventory Database**.
   a) Open **C:\091006Data\Managing Switchboards\Inventory Database.accdb**. If a security prompt is shown, select **Enable Content**.
   b) Save the file as *My Inventory Database.accdb*, and select **Enable Content** if you are prompted.

2. Add Switchboard Manager to the ribbon.
   a) Select **FILE→Options**.
   b) Select **Customize Ribbon**.
   c) Under **Main Tabs**, select **Create**, and then select **New Group**.

d) Select **Rename** and rename the item **Switchboard**, and then select **OK**.

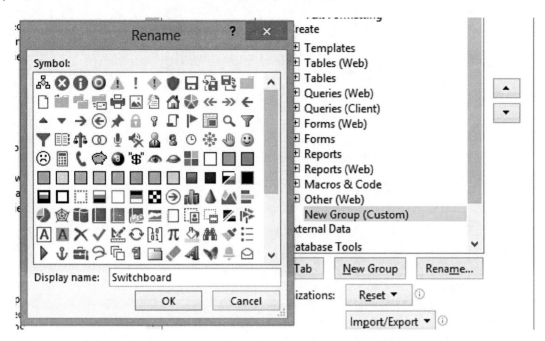

e) From the **Choose commands from** drop-down list, select **Commands Not in the Ribbon**.
f) Scroll down and select **Switchboard Manager**.

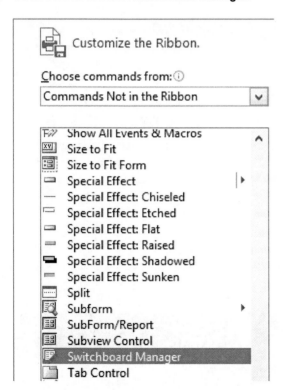

g) With the new **Switchboard (Custom)** group selected, select **Add**.
Switchboard Manager should appear under the **Switchboard (Custom)** item you created.

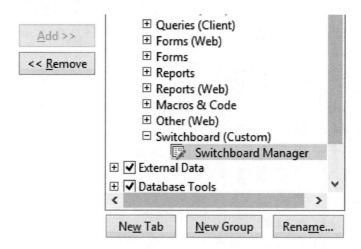

    h) Select **OK**.

3. Create a switchboard with an item to open the **frmInventory** form in Edit mode.
    a) Select **CREATE→Switchboard→Switchboard Manager**.
    b) Select **Yes** to confirm you would like to create a new switchboard.
    c) In the **Switchboard Manager** dialog box, select **Edit**.
    d) In the **Edit Switchboard Page** dialog box, select **New**.
    e) In the **Edit Switchboard Item** dialog box, in the **Text** text box, type *Inventory Form*
    f) From the **Command** drop-down list, select **Open Form in Edit Mode**.
    g) From the **Form** drop-down list, select **frmInventory**.

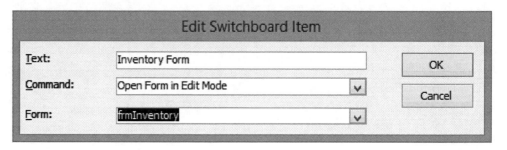

    h) Select **OK** to add the item to the switchboard.
    i) Select **Close** twice.

4. Test the switchboard.
    a) Open the **Switchboard** form in **Form** view.
    b) Select **Inventory Form** to open the **frmInventory** form.

    c) View the results, then close the **frmInventory** form.

TOPIC B

Modify a Database Switchboard

You used Switchboard Manager to create a basic switchboard form. You can use that same tool to make some edits to the switchboard. In this topic, you will modify the switchboard.

Switchboard Modification

You can modify the **Switchboard** form in **Design View** or by using the **Switchboard Manager**. However, you can only modify the switchboard's colors and layout in **Design View** or in **Layout View**. The **Switchboard Manager** allows you to create objects easily, but it has no design elements.

To modify the switchboard by adding, editing, or removing items, you use the **Switchboard Manager** and edit the existing switchboard.

To make your switchboard more visually appealing, you can change colors, extend the form's size, change fonts and much more. Use your imagination, but remember that visually, less is often more. Don't use too many colors, fonts, or design elements because it makes the form too busy and will have the opposite effect that you're looking for in a primary application interface, which is an efficient design with attractive color and layout.

To further enhance the look of your switchboard, or any form, you can add a background image. A background image can be as simple as a small graphic that you create with Microsoft Paint or something as elaborate as a photograph.

 Access the Checklist tile on your LogicalCHOICE course screen for reference information and job aids on How to Modify a Switchboard

ACTIVITY 6-2
Modifying a Switchboard

Before You Begin

My Inventory Database.accdb is open with the **Switchboard** form open.

Scenario

Your company has strong preferences that as many visual elements as possible adhere to the company's official colors. You decide that the switchboard you created should use the company colors, which are blue and red.

---

1. Change the background colors on the switchboard.
    a) View the **Switchboard** in **Design** view.
    b) In the **Form Header** section of the form, right-click the colored area and select **Fill/Back Color→Red**.
    c) In the **Detail** section, apply **Red** to the left section, and for the section of the form with the menu item, select **Blue**.

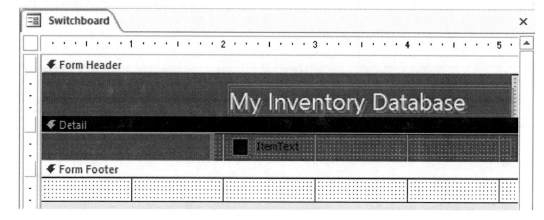

2. Save and test the form.
    a) Save the form.
    b) View the **Switchboard** in **Form** view.
        Notice that it is difficult to read the black text on the blue background.

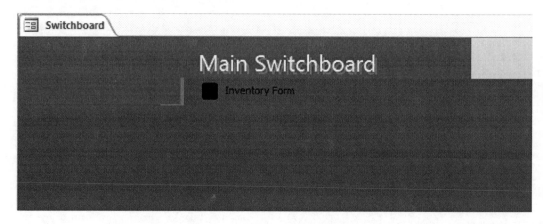

3. Change the font colors on the switchboard.
   a) View the **Switchboard** in **Design** view.
   b) Right-click the menu item text and select **Front/Fore Color**→**White**.

4. Save and test the form again.
   The text is more legible now that it is in a more contrasting color.

5. Close the form.

TOPIC C

Set Startup Options

An additional modification you might want to make to your database is to configure startup options. Startup options can help protect your database and make it easier for users to access forms, reports, and queries. In this topic, you will configure startup options for a database.

Database Startup Options

Setting Startup Options helps to further protect your database. In the Startup Options, you can title your database application, you can select a form to launch on database startup, and you can also hide the **Navigation** pane that contains your database objects (tables, forms, reports, queries, and macros).

Current Database Options

Startup Options are changed in the **Access Options** dialog box. Select **Current Database** in the left pane and then configure the options to suit your needs.

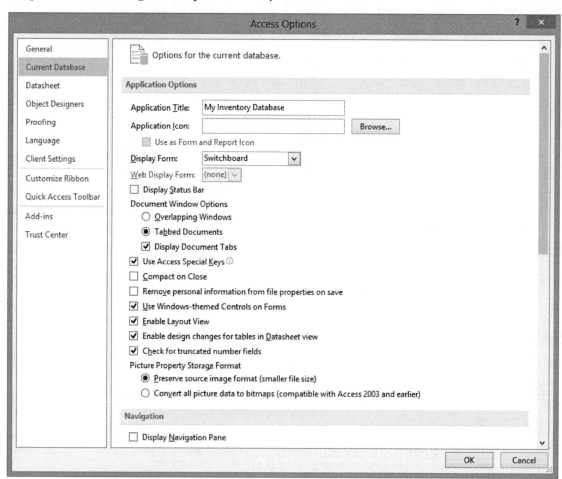

Figure 6–3: Startup Options.

 Note: If you need to make changes after you have set the startup options, hold **Shift** while opening the database.

Error Checking Options

You can set error checking options in the **Object Designers** section of the **Access Options** dialog box. These error checking options apply to all databases. Error checking is important for troubleshooting your database objects. The default is to have all error checking options selected.

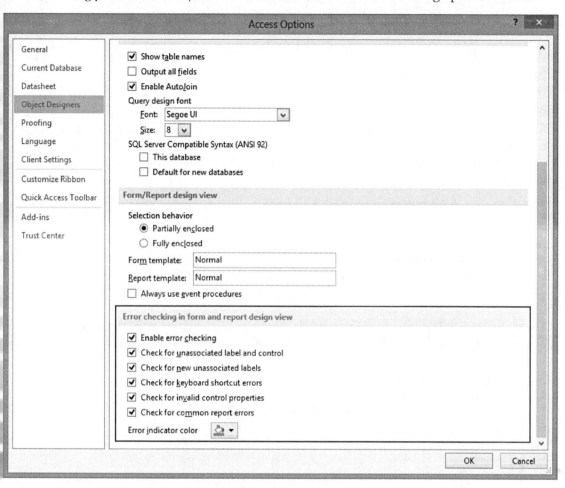

Figure 6-4: Error checking options for all databases.

Access the Checklist tile on your LogicalCHOICE course screen for reference information and job aids on **How to Set Startup Options**

ACTIVITY 6–3
Setting Startup Options

Before You Begin

My Inventory Database.accdb is open.

Scenario

You want to set further customizations on your database that make it more professional and hide certain elements that make up your database. General users don't need to tamper with or even know about many aspects of the database. You have decided to make some refinements to the Startup Options available to you.

1. Configure startup options for the My Inventory Database file.
   a) Select **FILE→Options**.
   b) Select **Current Database**.
   c) In the **Application Title** text box, type *My Inventory Database*
   d) From the **Display Form** drop-down list, select **Switchboard**.

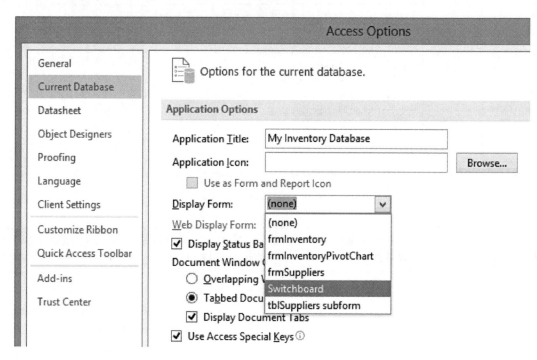

   e) Uncheck **Display Status Bar**.
   f) Uncheck **Display Navigation Pane**.
   g) Select **OK** to accept the changes to the startup options.
   h) In the message box, select **OK** to acknowledge that you need to close and reopen the database.

2. Test the changes.
   a) Close **My Inventory Database**.
   b) Reopen the **My Inventory Database**.
   c) Observe the database window.

There is no navigation pane or status bar. The database opened directly to the switchboard form you created.

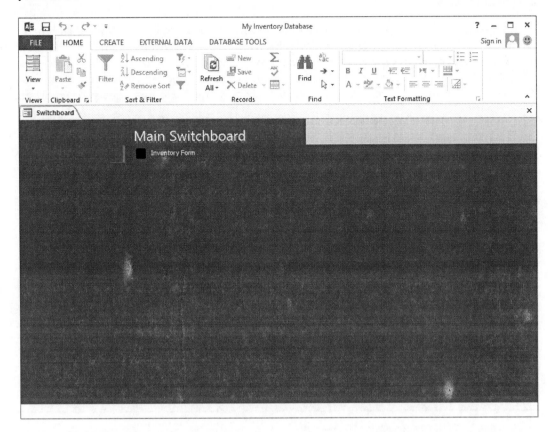

d) Close the **My Inventory Database** database.

Note: To learn how you can use your new Access skills, see the LearnTO **Identify Ways to Apply Your Access Skills** presentation from the **LearnTO** tile on the LogicalCHOICE Course screen.

Summary

In this lesson, you learned how to manage switchboards. You created a switchboard and then modified the design of the switchboard. You also configured the startup options for a database so that when a user opens the database, they see the switchboard. Using the switchboard can make it easier for users to find the database components they need to work with, and it also helps make the database more secure because users can't accidentally move or delete form, query, or report items.

Why should you create a switchboard for your database?

Why is switchboard design important?

 Note: To learn how you can sell the databases you create, see the LearnTO **Go Commercial with Your Databases** presentation from the **LearnTO** tile on the LogicalCHOICE Course screen.

 Note: Check your LogicalCHOICE Course screen for opportunities to interact with your classmates, peers, and the larger LogicalCHOICE online community about the topics covered in this course or other topics you are interested in. From the Course screen you can also access available resources for a more continuous learning experience.

Course Follow-Up

Well done! You've completed the *Microsoft® Office Access® 2013: Part 3* course. You have successfully created form controls, macros, subforms, and tab pages. You've learned how to manage a database, including backup, compact and repair, documentation, database splitting, encrypting a database, and adding a digital signature to a database. You've also learned how to create a switchboard for your database application.

What's Next?

You've reached the end of the Microsoft® Office Access® 2013 series but your learning shouldn't stop here. Logical Operations offers the entire Microsoft Office 2013 suite of applications for you to continue your studies.

You are encouraged to explore Access further by actively participating in any of the social media forums set up by your instructor or training administrator through the **Social Media** tile on the LogicalCHOICE Course screen.

A | Microsoft Office Access 2013 Exam 77–424

Selected Logical Operations courseware addresses Microsoft Office Specialist (MOS) certification skills for Microsoft Office 2013. The following table indicates where Access 2013 skills that are tested on Exam 77-424 are covered in the Logical Operations Microsoft Office Access 2013 series of courses.

Objective Domain	Covered In
1. Create and Manage a Database	
1.1. Create a New Database	
1.1.1. Create New Databases	Part 1
1.1.2. Create Databases Use Templates	Part 1
1.1.3. Create Databases in Older Formats	Part 1
1.1.4. Create Databases Use Wizards	Part 1
1.2. Manage Relationships and Keys	
1.2.1. Edit References Between Tables	Part 2
1.2.2. Create and Modify Relationships	Part 2
1.2.3. Set Primary Key Fields	Part 1
1.2.4. Enforce Referential Integrity	Part 2
1.2.5. Set Foreign Keys	Part 2
1.2.6. View Relationships	Part 2
1.3. Navigate Through a Database	
1.3.1. Navigate to Specific Records	Part 1
1.3.2. Set a Form as the Startup Option	Part 3, Topic 6-C
1.3.3. Use Navigation Forms	Part 3, Topic 1-D
1.3.4. Set Navigation Options	Part 3, Topic 6-C
1.3.5. Change Views	Part 3, Topic 3-A; Part 1
1.4. Protect and Maintain a Database	
1.4.1. Compact Databases	Part 3, Topic 4-B
1.4.2. Repair Databases	Part 3, Topic 4-B
1.4.3. Backup Databases	Part 3, Topic 4-B

Objective Domain	Covered In
1.4.4. Split Databases	Part 3, Topic 5-A
1.4.5. Encrypt Databases with a Password	Part 3, Topic 5-C
1.4.6. Merge Databases	Part 2
1.4.7. Recover Data From a Backup	Part 3, Topic 4-B
1.5. Print and Export a Database	
1.5.1. Print Reports	Part 1
1.5.2. Print Records	Part 1
1.5.3. Maintain Backward Compatibility	Part 1
1.5.4. Save Databases as Templates	Part 3, Topic 5-D
1.5.5. Save Databases to External Locations	Part 2
1.5.6. Export to Alternate Formats	Part 2
2. Build Tables	
2.1. Create a Table	
2.1.1. Create New Tables	Part 1
2.2.1. Import External Data Into Tables	Part 3, Topic 4-A
2.1.2. Create Linked Tables from External Sources	Part 3, Topic 4-A
2.1.3. Import Tables from Other Databases	Part 2
2.1.4. Create Tables from Templates and Application Parts	Part 3, Topic 5-D; Part 1
2.1.5. Freeze or Unfreeze fields	Part 1
2.2. Format a Table	
2.2.1. Hide Fields in Tables	Part 1
2.2.2. Change Data Formats	Part 1
2.2.3. Add Total Rows	Part 1
2.2.4. Add Table Descriptions	Part 2
2.2.5. Rename Tables	Part 1
2.3. Manage Records	
2.3.1. Update Records	Part 1; Part 2
2.3.2. Add New Records	Part 1
2.3.3. Delete Records	Part 1
2.3.4. Append Records from External Data	Part 1
2.3.5. Find and Replace Data	Part 1
2.3.6. Sort Records	Part 1
2.3.7. Filter Records	Part 1
2.3.8. Group Records	Part 1
2.4. Create and Modify Fields	
2.4.1. Add Fields to Tables	Part 1

Objective Domain	Covered In
2.4.2. Add Validation Rules to Fields	Part 2
2.4.3. Change Field Captions	Part 3, Topic 2-A
2.4.4. Change Field Sizes	Part 2
2.4.5. Change Field Data Types	Part 1
2.4.6. Configure Fields to Auto-Increment	Part 1
2.4.7. Set Default Values	Part 2
2.4.8. Use Input Masks	Part 2
2.4.9. Delete Fields	Part 1
3. Create Queries	
3.1. Create a Query	
3.1.1. Run Queries	Part 1
3.1.2. Create Crosstab Queries	Part 1
3.1.3. Create Parameter Queries	Part 1
3.1.4. Create Action Queries	Part 1
3.1.5. Create Multi-Table Queries	Part 1
3.1.6. Save Queries	Part 1
3.1.7. Delete Queries	Part 1
3.2. Modify a Query	
3.2.1. Rename Queries	Part 1
3.2.2. Add New Fields	Part 1
3.2.3. Remove Fields	Part 1
3.2.4. Hide Fields	Part 1
3.2.5. Sort Data within Queries	Part 1
3.2.6. Format Fields within Queries	
3.3. Utilize Calculated Fields and Grouping within a Query	
3.3.1. Add Calculated Fields	Part 1
3.3.2. Add Conditional Logic	Part 1
3.3.3. Group and Summarize Data	Part 1
3.3.4. Use Comparison Operators	Part 1
3.3.5. Use Basic Operators	Part 1
4. Create Forms	
4.1. Create a Form	
4.1.1. Create New Forms	Part 1
4.1.2. Create Forms with Application Parts	Part 3, Topic 1-A
4.1.3. Save Forms	Part 1
4.1.4. Delete Forms	Part 1

Objective Domain	Covered In
4.2. Set Form Controls	
4.2.1. Move Form Controls	Part 1
4.2.2. Add Form Controls	Part 1
4.2.3. Modify Data Sources	Part 3, Topic 4-A
4.2.4. Remove Form Controls	Part 2
4.2.5. Set Form Control Properties	Part 1
4.2.6. Manage Labels	Part 3, Topic 1-A
4.3. Format a Form	
4.3.1. Modify Tab Order in Forms	Part 3, Topic 1-A
4.3.2. Format Print Layouts	Part 1
4.3.3. Sort Records	Part 1
4.3.4. Apply Themes	Part 1
4.3.5. Change Margins	Part 1
4.3.6. Insert Backgrounds	Part 3, Topic 6-B
4.3.7. Auto-Order Forms	Part 3, Topic 1-A
4.3.8. Insert Headers and Footers	Part 1
4.3.9. Insert Images	Part 3, Topic 6-B
4.3.10. Modify Existing Forms	Part 3, Topics 1-A. 6-A
5. Create Reports	
5.1. Create a Report	
5.1.1. Create new Reports	Part 1
5.1.2. Create Reports with Application Parts	Part 3, Topic 5-D
5.1.3. Delete Reports	Part 1
5.2. Set Report Controls	
5.2.1. Group Data by Fields	Part 1; Part 2
5.2.2. Sort Data	Part 1
5.2.3. Add Sub-Forms	Part 2
5.2.4. Modify Data Sources	Part 1
5.2.5. Add Report Controls	Part 2
5.2.6. Manage Labels	Part 1
5.3. Format a Report	
5.3.1. Format Reports into Multiple Columns	
5.3.2. Add Calculated Fields	Part 2
5.3.3. Set Margins	Part 1; Part 2
5.3.4. Add Backgrounds	Part 2
5.3.5. Change Report Orientation	Part 2

Objective Domain	Covered In
5.3.6. Change Sort Order	Part 1
5.3.7. Insert Headers and Footers	Part 1
5.3.8. Insert Images	Part 1
5.3.9. Insert Page Numbers	Part 2
5.3.10. Apply Themes	Part 1
5.3.11. Modify Existing Reports	Part 1; Part 2

B Microsoft Access 2013 Common Keyboard Shortcuts

The following table lists common keyboard shortcuts you can use in Access 2013.

Function	Shortcut
Open a new database	Ctrl + N
Open an existing database	Ctrl + O
Open the **Print** dialog box	Ctrl + P
Open the **Find** tab	Ctrl + F
Copy the selected contents	Ctrl + C
Cut the selected contents	Ctrl + X
Paste the selected content	Ctrl + V
Undo typing	Ctrl + Z
Cycle between open windows	Ctrl + F6
Check spelling	F7
Rename a selected object	F2
Show the access keys	F10
Switch to the next tab in a dialog box	Ctrl + Tab
Switch to the previous tab in a dialog box	Ctrl + Shift + Tab
Move to the beginning of an entry	Home
Move to the end of an entry	End
Toggle the property sheet tab	F4
Toggle the **Field List** pane	Alt + F8
Insert the current data	Ctrl + ;
Insert the current time	Ctrl + Shift + :
Add a new record	Ctrl + +
Delete the current record	Ctrl + -
Save changes to the current record	Shift + Enter

Lesson Labs

Lesson labs are provided for certain lessons as additional learning resources for this course. Lesson labs are developed for selected lessons within a course in cases when they seem most instructionally useful as well as technically feasible. In general, labs are supplemental, optional unguided practice and may or may not be performed as part of the classroom activities. Your instructor will consider setup requirements, classroom timing, and instructional needs to determine which labs are appropriate for you to perform, and at what point during the class. If you do not perform the labs in class, your instructor can tell you if you can perform them independently as self-study, and if there are any special setup requirements.

Lesson Lab 1–1
Creating a Close Form Command Button

Activity Time: 30 minutes

Data Files

C:\091006Data\Implementing Advanced Form Design\LabDatabase.accdb

Scenario

You need to create a suppliers form, and then add a command button to it that closes the form.

---

1. Open the **LabDatabase.accdb** and select **Enable Content** if prompted.

2. Save the database as *My LabDatabase.accdb* and select **Enable Content** if prompted.

3. Create a form from the **tblSuppliers** table.

4. Add a **Close Form** button to the form.

5. Save the form as *frmSuppliers*

6. Test your work by using the **Close Form** button to close the form.

7. Close the database.

Lesson Lab 4-1
Linking to an External Data Source

Activity Time: 20 minutes

Data Files

C:\091006Data\Using Advanced Database Management\LabDatabase.accdb

Scenario

You learn that an update to the product data will be released weekly through an Excel spreadsheet. Rather than having to copy and paste this data each time it is updated, you decide to link the spreadsheet directly to your database as the data source, so it will update automatically each time the database is opened.

---

1. Open the **LabDatabase.accdb** and select **Enable Content** if prompted.

2. Save the database as *LabExternal.accdb* and select **Enable Content** if prompted.

3. Delete the **tblProducts** table from the database.

4. Link to the Excel spreadsheet, **tblProducts.xlsx**, as an external data source.

5. Open the **tblProducts** table to see the data.

6. Close the table and the database.

Lesson Lab 5-1
Splitting a Database

Activity Time: 30 minutes

Data Files

C:\091006Data\Distributing and Securing a Database\LabDatabase.accdb

Scenario

The LabDatabase.accdb is ready for multi-user access but the only components that will be used are the tables. The lab database is going to be used as a back end for a web database. The query and reports will be kept for reference in the new web application. Split the database to prepare it for hand off to the web development team.

1. Open the **LabDatabase.accdb**, and select **Enable Content** if prompted.

2. Save the back-end database as *My LabDatabase_be.accdb*

3. Close the database.

Glossary

action
Programmatic steps performed by a macro. For example: Open a form.

arguments
A parameter given to a macro to perform an action upon. For example: Inventory form.

conditions
A filter in a Macro. Example: [Field1] > [Field2].

control
A database object on a form or report that performs some task. For example: a command button that closes a form.

data validation
Restrictions that limit user choices and restrict opportunities to introduce incorrect entries into a database. For example: Limiting choices to a drop-down list of options.

Datepicker
The Access 2013 replacement for the **Calendar** control. The Datepicker is an active control that provides an interactive calendar object from which a user may pick a date to be used on a form or report.

digital certificate
To create a digital signature, you have to have a signing certificate, which proves identity.

digital signature
An electronic, encrypted stamp of authentication. A signature confirms that the information originated from the signer and has not been altered.

event
An action performed by a user on a form that triggers a corresponding action by the database. For example, tabbing from one field to another triggers an event to check data validity.

exclusive mode
A method of opening an Access database so that only one person has access to the database for maintenance purposes.

Expression Builder
The part of the Macro Builder where the database designer enters equations and field names usually associated with data validation.

external data source
Any data that does not reside inside the Access database. For example: An Excel file.

input mask
A data validation technique setup to guide the user in entering the correct data for a field.

macro
A program within Access that performs a series of defined actions.

Macro Builder

The editor where a database designer constructs macro actions into a functioning macro.

object dependency

Database entities (objects) rely on one another for data. These relationships are known as dependencies.

subform

A form that is placed inside another form usually to display a limited amount of data in a datasheet style format.

Switchboard

A special Access form that uses built-in controls to open other forms, reports or to close the application.

tab order

The top-to-bottom, left-to-right sequence of moving from one form field to another.

Tab Pages

A special form that separates information into multiple pages in a tabbed format.

Trust Center

The location within Access where a database designer manages security and privacy of the database and its components.

trusted location

A folder on a local or network disk that is recognized by Access as being safe to load content from without passing through Trust Center checks.

Index